Praise for

"The reflections in this eloquent a[n]... ...ant insights for anyone interested i[n] ...experiences of armed conflict, survival in prison and refugee camps, the strength of family, myriad aspects of cross-cultural adjustment—and the profound power of education."

—**Stephanie Farrior**, Professor of Law and Director,
Center for Applied Human Rights, Vermont Law School

"Joseph Kaifala's *Adamalui* is a stunning spiritual memoir about one man's journey, not just through the harrowing terrain of civil war, but into the depths of his soul. An inspiring achievement."

—**Flor Edwards**, author of *Apocalypse Child: A Life in End Times*

"*Adamalui* by Joseph Kaifala is perhaps the best book to capture the essence of Sierra Leone's history between 1990 and 2004. This exemplary work of art written from Joseph's life takes us through an experience of living in a prison as a child in war torn Liberia, making the best of life in a refugee camp as a youth in Guinea and enduring a brutal rebel war in Sierra Leone. Joseph brings us into his life, and consequently most Sierra Leonean youth, with careful detail and purposeful sense of humor used excellently to lighten often heavy topics. I could relate to many parts of the story because like Joseph, I went to RCNUWC and then the US after taking my WASSCE in Freetown. However, the combination of particular experiences which make this memoir a spectacular work could only be Joseph's. This book leaves me hopeful for Sierra Leone because even though its stories are based in the past, it features many young people, including Joseph and his brother Francis, who are already impacting society in education and civic life. What a blessing that Joseph chose to share his story!!! It's the best account of our generation out there."

—**David Sengeh, PhD**, 2018 TED Senior Fellow

ADAMALUI

**A Survivor's Journey from Civil Wars
in Africa to Life in America**

JOSEPH KAIFALA

TURNER

Turner Publishing Company
Nashville, Tennessee
New York, New York
www.turnerpublishing.com

Cover design: Maddie Cothren
Book design: Tim Holtz

Library of Congress Cataloging-in-Publication Data
Names: Kaifala, Joseph, author.
Title: Adamalui : a survivor's journey from civil wars in Africa to life in
  America / Joseph Kaifala.
Description: Nashville, Tennessee : Turner, 2018.
Identifiers: LCCN 2017054005 (print) | LCCN 2018002587 (ebook) | ISBN
  9781681626857 (e-book) | ISBN 9781681626833 (pbk. : alk. paper)
Subjects: LCSH: Kaifala, Joseph. | Sierra Leone--History--Civil War,
  1991-2002--Personal narratives. | Liberia--History--Civil War,
  1989-1996--Personal narratives. | Sierra Leoneans--United
  States--Biography. | Refugees--Sierra Leone--Biography. | Refugees--United
  States--Biography. | United States--Emigration and immigration--Government
  policy.
Classification: LCC DT516.828.K35 (ebook) | LCC DT516.828.K35 A3 2018 (print)
  | DDC 966.4/0441 [B] --dc23
LC record available at https://lccn.loc.gov/2017054005

Printed in the United States of America
18 19 20 21   10 9 8 7 6 5 4 3 2 1

In memory of
Ben M. Kaifala

ADAMALUI

PROLOGUE

There is no mountain so high we cannot
climb. It is merely a matter of time.

After years of living in Norway and the United States, I am
beginning to think that I was just lucky. I am an ordinary
person who has lived a fortunate life, some of which I orchestrated,
but most of the time I've had to navigate without a compass. The
events in my life have happened in such a way that I sometimes
wonder who is in control. I feel as though I have been wandering
in fields of supernatural occurrences where things transpire beyond
my comprehension. Such happenings are good luck when they are
favorable and bad luck when they are the opposite. Muslims and
Christians have similar references to good and bad luck, except they
let God or Satan decide the outcome of life events. Luck itself is
a god for the nonreligious, or for those who are content with an
undefined supernatural. But many years of religious education and
the events of my life during the Liberian and Sierra Leonean civil
wars will simply not allow me to place my entire life's burden on
God. Sometimes I can't help but think that God has better things
to do and he is simply not interested in the soap opera of my life.
But even if he should be bothered at all, I consider myself too far
down his to-do list.

My Sunday school lessons taught me the association between
good and evil, God and Satan. The equation is simple: good and
favorable equal God; evil and unfavorable equal Satan. Yet these
very equations have become blurred in my life after so many years
of struggle for survival. It appears that in the battle between good

and evil, evil has the upper hand and God is indifferent. The extent of human wretchedness has led Archbishop Desmond Tutu, the living moral spine of Africa, to lament that "if God ever wanted to consider the folly of having created us, we have provided him ample cause to do so." But how can I truly understand what God's intentions are? He says in Isaiah, "For my thoughts are not your thoughts, neither are your ways my ways. . . . For as the heavens are higher than the earth, so are my ways higher than your ways and my thoughts than your thoughts" (Isaiah 55:8–9).

The elders of my Mende ethnic group in Sierra Leone often admonish us that it is impossible for an *adamalui*, a child of Adam, to understand the ways of God. Everything happens according to God's will, and all sentient beings are obliged to live within this principle and to follow God's commandments. Just as the heavens are higher than the earth, so too are the ways of God higher than our ways, and no one on earth is perfect on the scale of divine judgment. "For all have sinned, and come short of the glory of God" (Romans 3:23). But God has his kingdom, and man has inherited the earth. The Kingdom of God is presumably higher than the Kingdom of the World, and the Lord comes not for those who think they are righteous and worthy of his grace, but for those who know they are sinners and need repentance. My conundrum is that some days I feel as righteous as an archangel, and other days I cannot convince myself of the presence of even a fiber of virtue in the bundle of sins I carry.

I am now standing at the intersection of the Kingdom of the World and the Kingdom of God, and I know not which way to go. It seems as if I am not even directing myself on this crossroad. The Kingdom of the World urges me to believe that reality is here on earth and I am the author of my being. But even though I may be able to write the script of my life, I do not have much control over the activities of the universe. Whether I wish it or not, morning comes and night falls. The Kingdom of God requires a leap of faith in which I accept that God has always been in charge of my survival. But God has become an enigma to me. What kind of God wants to be on full-time duty, making sure that people are good? If such a God exists, wouldn't we all be as virtuous as we can be? Like a manufacturer who separates defective products from satisfactory ones, or a farmer who uproots weeds from grains, God, if he is God, has the power to eliminate evil and strike out ill fortune. If this is not so, I can no longer be sure that my life fits within the equation of good and evil, good luck and bad luck.

I now have enough time to ponder these questions without bullets and rocket-propelled grenades flying over my head. There was no time during the wars in Liberia and Sierra Leone to think twice about anything. The pragmatic maneuver for those who believed in God was to pray while on the run and searching for a hideout. After all, even the rebels prayed to God during their destruction, rape, and slaughter of innocent people. The rebels usually recited both the Lord's Prayer and the *fatir* before heading to the front line to let loose unimaginable barbarity on civilians. There is a popular saying among Liberians and Sierra Leoneans: "God helps those who help themselves." Religious leaders often used a tale titled "The Believer" to illustrate the idea that God's ways are higher than ours:

A long time ago, a pious man lived in a village situated in a valley. He was so devout that other residents called him the Believer. His whole community loved him and admired his devotion to God. He was the wisest man in the valley. People came to him for advice on many issues, from farming to the teachings of the Bible. He always had precise answers for everyone.

One year there was a flood in the valley, and everyone was told to leave for higher ground. Rain fell day and night, and the two rivers surrounding the village overflowed and consumed the town. Chaos ensued as everyone ran for dear life. All inhabitants were evacuated except the Believer. He would not leave his house because he believed that God would come to his rescue.

Everyone who went by offered to escort the Believer to higher ground because they loved him and would not let him drown. "I have faith in God and know that he will come to my rescue at the right hour," he shouted to people who offered to help him evacuate. The Believer was very sure that God would never forsake him; God would save him just like he had saved Noah from the mighty flood. But the Believer's community of friends would not give up on trying to persuade him to flee.

As the floodwater rose and covered the roads, making them impassable for most cars, a man in a truck stopped at the Believer's house and knocked on the door. "Hurry, your holiness!" he shouted. "The water is rising fast! Come with me to higher ground; you don't have much time!" But the Believer replied, "Go away, ye of little faith! Have I not told you countless times that God always comes to the aid of his people?" The Believer continued to pray; he would not leave his house unless God came to his rescue.

A few hours after the man in the truck left, the water rose several feet more, completely flooding the Believer's house. He climbed onto the kitchen table and continued to recite his Holy Rosary. He was determined to wait for God. Just as the water was reaching his knees, another man in a boat rowed over to the kitchen window and shouted, "Your holiness, get in my boat! I will rescue you."

"No!" the Believer shouted back. "Do not interrupt my prayers any further; only God Almighty can deliver me from this flood."

The floodwater rose and rose, and soon the only option left for the pious man was to climb up to the roof of his house. The rain continued to fall, and the entire land was covered with water. There was no one left in the village except the Believer, who was now staggering on the roof of his house, praying to God for help. Just as he was about to complete the last Hail Mary of his Holy Rosary, he looked up and saw a helicopter above his head. A ladder was lowered. The pilot was Ishmael, a good friend of the Believer.

"Get on! Get on! Get on!" Ishmael shouted until his voice faded.

"Get away from me!" the Believer shouted back. "Do not blow me off the roof! My God, the God of Abraham, will deliver me."

Ishmael tried over and over to convince his friend to climb up the ladder, but the stubborn pious man would not listen. Ishmael, on the other hand, could not wait forever; the storm was getting severe and the rain was falling harder. He left the Believer on his chimney, holding tight and still praying for God to rescue him. The water eventually rose to his neck, and he perished in the flood.

When the Believer arrived at the Hall of Judgment, he immediately requested to speak to God. Saint Peter led the Believer to the throne of God Almighty.

The Believer kneeled and said, "My Lord and my God, I prayed fervently for the rain to stop and for you to rescue me from the flood, but you left me there to drown. Why did you forsake me?"

"Hurry not to accusations, my child," said the Lord. "I sent you a truck, a boat, and a helicopter, but you were adamant. Finally, I had to let you die. For though you are pious, you do not understand my ways."

Unlike the Believer, during the tumultuous days of our struggles for survival, Sierra Leoneans and Liberians had to make use of the first option that came our way, whether it came from God or not. In my case, if it has been God all this while, then *which* God? For the Mano River Union of Sierra Leone, Guinea, Liberia, and Ivory Coast is a region of many Gods. Is it the God of my grandmother, of the Friday prayers, and of the Islamic school I attended when I was a boy? Or is it the God of my parents, the one hanging from a cross, to whom my parents often whispered, "Our Father, who art in heaven"? Could it be the God of my ancestors, to whom my other grandmother poured libations? The God who was present when my family gathered to name a child, bless a marriage, or bury the dead? Whichever God he is, my people believe he can do no evil, so I cannot blame him for the years when I prayed for him to take control of my life and grant me each day my bread and deliver me from evil while I remained hungry and surrounded by wickedness. Maybe he was there with me, and that is why I am seated here today writing these stories. Perhaps I am just lucky. India's Mahatma Gandhi pointed out that one's denial of divine law does not liberate him from its operation. God is God whether we believe in him or not, and he protects his chosen ones.

But if God was not protecting me and I am just surviving on good luck, why am *I* the one meriting this good luck when so many children have perished and more are still dying in Sierra Leone, Guinea, and Liberia? Is luck itself susceptible to selectivity? Why would any luck or God not favor a child like Memuna Mansaray, who at the very tender age of two got her right hand amputated after being shot by rebels in Sierra Leone? What about the thousands more who were transformed by drugs and lack of options into killers or child soldiers? When children witness the massacre of their parents and the rape of their sisters, there can be no other rational option but revenge. This is why many children took up arms in Sierra Leone and Liberia: to prolong their own survival and pursue the unknown killers of their families.

I could have been one of the children fighting that invisible enemy. If I had joined them, I might have lived, or maybe my young bones would have been added to the manure upon which new nations now grow. Those were the days when the idea of death was a comfort, and we all awaited the moment when it would come, be it by AK-47 or starvation, and we would depart from this earth unknown and unaccounted for, like the thousands of civilians who died in the jungles of Sierra Leone, Guinea, and Liberia. Like the innocent civilians who still reappear in my vision as I saw them some years ago underneath the burning sun when I had to jump over their corpses to pick bananas. But it must have been God who placed the bananas there for me to eat; he took me there in the first place. It could have been me rotting and baking beneath the burning sun. Instead, I am the witness, the one who is telling this story more than twenty-five years later.

Life seems so different than it was a quarter century ago that I can reflect on the journey that took me out of war-ravaged Liberia and Sierra Leone to Norway and the United States. I know not where this journey is leading me, but as my mother used to say, "If you do not know where you are going, you must at least remember where you came from." Like an antelope that has broken through a bush trap, I know from whence I come. I am still moving forward even as you read these writings, but the road is different, and the goal, whatever it may be, is attainable. Be it fortuitous or by the grace of God, I have done my share in conducting this train to the station where it now stands en route to another. There is a lot to write about my life during those years of war, but as Elie Wiesel has said, no witness is capable of telling the whole story. This is not a story about what I went through; it is a story of how I got here.

CHAPTER 1

There will be no heaven greater than the love we share on earth.

At about the age of six, I moved from Sierra Leone to Liberia to live with my father, who was a teacher at St. Joseph's Catholic School in Voinjama, Lofa County. My father had had to leave us in Sierra Leone to find work in Liberia. At the time, two former soldiers, Joseph Momoh and Samuel Doe, were presidents of Sierra Leone and Liberia respectively. Momoh, who became president through a sham referendum in 1985, was handpicked by his predecessor, Siaka Stevens. Doe officially became president in 1985 by rigging a sham multiparty election. He was a master sergeant of the Armed Forces of Liberia when he led a coup d'état in 1980 against President William R. Tolbert, Jr., ending 133 years of Americo-Liberian rule. Americo-Liberians are descendants of the African-Americans who were first resettled in Liberia in the 1820s by the American Colonization Society (ACS), an organization founded by Rev. Robert Finley, Bushrod Washington, Henry Clay, John Randolph of Virginia, Elias B. Caldwell, Francis Scott Key, Daniel Webster, and other influential Americans for the manumission of American slaves and their resettlement in Liberia. The organization is reported to have transported approximately twelve thousand African-Americans to Liberia. By the time I moved from Sierra Leone to Liberia, both countries were on the verge of sociopolitical shambles resulting from poor governance, food shortages, price hikes, school shutdowns, lack of health care, harassment of opposition leaders, youth unemployment, and rumors of arms caches along the border separating the two countries.

I was on my own most of the time because my father was often busy with school and private tutorials. I woke up one morning in what used to be a peaceful country and there was war. Suddenly schools and offices were closed; blood was everywhere. I was too young to understand why people who had been good neighbors the day before had overnight become enemies willing to massacre each other in cold blood, but whatever the war was about, in my child's mind I was happy because I had a day off from school, and another day, and more days—until I was tired of days off. When the war eventually reached Voinjama, I understood very quickly that these were no ordinary days off, as guns roared outside and my father urged me to keep my head flat on the floor. Bullets were hitting the building, and the debris of mud bricks was falling on us. This is when I became a man.

As I now reflect on those years, after a decade of school in the United States, I nod my head and say, "Life is struggle." I have overcome hopelessness and transformed my life into something within my control. Surviving the war and living in the United States are two different journeys in my life, even though they have been happening along the same path, with a forward-pointing compass. The day-to-day struggles of escaping death and enduring hunger were often out of my control, but diligence and perseverance are two virtues I possessed, especially when it seemed possible that I might live for another day. *If tomorrow finds me alive*, I thought, *I must have something to show for it.* Something to convince whoever was in control that I deserved to live one more day, or perhaps many more years. As the German philosopher Friedrich Nietzsche wrote, "If we have our own *why* in life, we shall get along with almost any *how*." When life offers no present meaning, a promising future may become a major ingredient for survival. As Viktor Frankl, the father of logotherapy, declared, "Woe to him who saw no more sense in his life, no aim, no purpose, and therefore no point in carrying on. He [is] soon lost." Even in moments of extreme suffering, one must hold on to a ray of light that points toward the future.

The pursuit of education motivated me to live each day. It was clear to me at an early age that if I survived the war, I would need more than just life. Maybe even this idea is a divine gift of having a caring father who prepared me for the future by instilling the value of education in me. But the choice was mine. I was the one who chose to read whatever brown pages I could lay my hands on during those years of war. I chose to go to school on a hungry belly in refugee camps, and I chose to swallow many insults and humiliations to stay in school. I don't know why education seemed so important to me; maybe it was simply another means of keeping hope alive, but I could not think of anything better. In the same circumstances, my siblings did no less. The first time a rocket was fired on my hometown, Pendembu, as we were again getting ready to flee, my younger brother, Francis, turned around amid the confusion and in tears asked my mother, "Ngor Tewa, mui ya lema skui hun?" Sister Tewa—this is what he calls our mother—will we no longer be going to school? Francis loved school, and he never wanted a day off.

My mother was at a loss as to how to explain to my brother that he couldn't attend school, and moreover that he would have to leave his house to hide in the jungle. He might even get killed. This is what made my mother cry—the thought of being unable to protect her children from brutes and merciless killers. My father and I had nothing to add. We had just returned to Sierra Leone from Liberia, where we had witnessed the misery of war, and we knew exactly how bad it could get. My father simply placed his hands on my head and said, "Mister Man, we are running again." I started to cry. But we had very little time to cry. We had to leave Pendembu as quickly as possible. It was never safe to be in town the first time there was a rebel attack. Most of the rape, chopping off of limbs, looting, and massacre happened during the first attack, when towns and villages were transformed into blood pools and heaven closed its door to the wailing of the innocent.

The wailing of the innocent. I heard it in Freetown in 1999 when I attended the Sierra Leone Grammar School (SLGS) after the January 6 rebel invasion of the city. There was so much dread in Freetown that religious ministers and radio talk-show hosts one day asked surviving residents to go outside at six p.m. and shout the name of Jesus until the city shook. I went out that evening, not to shout, but to see and hear what would happen. At the appointed time, people started to yell "Jesus!" from all corners of the city, producing a roar that made the entire city tremble. In my skepticism, I couldn't help but mumble, "Where has he been all these years, if he truly cares about us?" I immediately thought of my devout mother and regretted thinking out loud. My mother always prays for her children, and deep down I felt that somehow God must have a plan for my life.

"Jesus," I muttered.

How else could I have survived all those years away from my mother? How else could I have learned anything in school? On some school days, it took me several minutes to even realize that a teacher was in the classroom, either because of the chilling silence that had befallen Freetown after the 1999 rebel incursion, or because of the extreme hunger I felt. There were days when I got so hungry that my eyesight became fuzzy and I could hear tingling sounds in my ears. Sometimes I was revivified only when a kind friend offered me a piece of *oleleh*, pounded beans mixed with condiments and boiled in banana leaves, or *akara*, pounded beans fried with spices. But what really saved my life in those days was the availability of cheap *gari*, ground and dried cassava that can be soaked in water and eaten with sugar. Those were also the days when I had the choice of staying in school or going down to the nearby Murray Town wharf in western Freetown to find a job on one of the Spanish fishing boats. I chose to remain in school as long as I could, and that decision has brought me this far.

Every turn in life affords its own struggles, its own dilemmas. I wake up today surrounded by the wealth of the United States, thinking of my compatriots still struggling to make life worth living in Sierra Leone and Liberia. Sometimes I think it is for them that I survived those years when I should have died, the years when I could have given up and taken another path, the years when other children lay in ambush, waiting for the enemy to show up, an enemy who, like them, was a foot soldier in a futile revolution. In my service to the poor, I am often invigorated by the fact that some years ago I was one of the people I now serve. But whatever the fortune is that keeps smiling on me, I am grateful to God for giving me the good luck to become an instrument of peace and inspiration to some. If the preacher of the Old Testament is right, "The race is not to the swift, nor the battle to the strong, neither yet bread to the wise, nor yet riches to men of understanding, nor yet favor to men of skill" (Ecclesiastes 9:11). It is by timing and chance that we are steered toward good luck or bad luck, God or Satan.

At such a young age I had no way to make meaning of what I went through. I am still trying to understand most of my experiences, especially those that occurred between 1990 and 1991, when I was imprisoned with my father in Liberia. Charles Taylor, leader of the National Patriotic Front of Liberia (NPFL), had been frustrated by a split in his revolutionary forces, and although a majority of the rebels remained in his camp, many joined one of his former commanders, Prince Johnson, to form a new branch of the NPFL, the Independent National Patriotic Front of Liberia (INPFL). The Economic Community of West African States (ECOWAS) intervened in the Liberian conflict by deploying its peacekeeping force, the Economic Community of West African States Monitoring Group (ECOMOG). The conflict became a four-way battle between Taylor, Johnson, Doe, and ECOMOG. Samuel Doe successfully stood his ground and made the executive mansion impregnable. As the factions clashed in various quarters of Monrovia, ECOMOG dropped bombs on strategic locations, especially targeting Taylor's rebels.

Sierra Leone is the most strategically positioned neighbor to Liberia, which made Lungi International Airport, outside Freetown, an appropriate base for ECOMOG. Sierra Leone was also one of the countries contributing troops to ECOMOG, which Taylor viewed as a form of connivance against his revolution, a betrayal he was determined to punish. Taylor had visited Freetown before launching his rebellion to ask President Joseph Momoh for support and permission to use Sierra Leonean territory as a base. President Momoh rejected Taylor's request and briefly detained him in Freetown. Corrupt politicians in Momoh's administration extorted money from Taylor for his freedom. Taylor was infuriated by the treatment, and he promised Sierra Leone a bitter taste of war. Sierra Leone's participation in the ECOWAS mission worsened the situation.

Sunday church services in Voinjama became the most interesting activity for civilians during the war. We prayed for the war to end and sang touching hymns in exaggerated voices, often shouting above our lungs. It was evident that the words of songs we previously had sung without much effort acquired new meaning. The responsorial Psalm 143 "O Lord, Hear My Prayer" was recited louder than usual.

Church was where adults caught up on recent news and exchanged information about where to acquire rice or palm oil. Children were allowed to run around the mission, utilizing well-needed playtime. Sundays were also when bad news was disseminated among congregants. When the priest received credible information about parishioners who had been killed, he prayed for their souls, mentioning each person by name. During Universal Prayer, church members prayed for friends or neighbors who had been killed.

Things were relatively safe for the remaining residents of Voinjama until one Sunday when everything took a turn for the worse, especially for foreigners. Taylor issued an order instructing his rebels to arrest and detain West Africans living in Liberia. The news did not make it through the underground information channels beforehand. Had it spread, perhaps some people might have escaped before the rebels got to them. Patrick, an uncle my father had invited to Voinjama, went to visit some friends after mass one Sunday and was picked up. News of Patrick's arrest did not reach us until later that evening. My father was relieved to hear that Patrick was detained and not dead.

My father woke up early the following day. Mr. Jamiru, who would later marry my sister Doris, was up, too. Instead of waiting to be arrested, my father and Mr. Jamiru decided to surrender to the rebels. The rebels usually brutalized their victims during arrest, and my father thought they could avoid such violence by surrendering. More importantly, he wanted to see Patrick and make sure he was still alive. We boiled potatoes for breakfast and ate in an unusual silence. My father, an already stoic Mende man, spoke little when he had to deal with complex emotions. His calculations took place in his mind. Brainstorming with others was not his preferred approach to problem solving. He was a silent thinker who mentally joggled his ideas before proposing them aloud. Relatives often misconstrued his silence to mean a lack of interest, and my mother had to defend his reserve. My father was, however, a deeply calculative and sentimental man who brought love and care to every situation. Patience is one virtue he possessed more than most people.

After our breakfast, my father and Mr. Jamiru got ready to meet the rebels. I was not involved in any of the preparations. African parents do not usually make children part of their deliberation, even when the issue at hand concerns the child. Unlike what I have seen in many Western homes, my parents never asked what I thought of any matter. The adults made the decisions, and we children obeyed. Years later, reflecting on that day, I would find it interesting that my father dressed formally to meet with rebels who, at best, wore rags adorned with talismanic ornaments, strings of human body parts, or newly looted 2Pac T-shirts bearing the phrase "All Eyez on Me." Maybe my father never thought he would be detained; after all, what had he done? Some parents would have told their child something profound or at least emotional before embarking on a perilous journey, in this case surrendering to ragtag rebels who killed at whim, but my father was not a man of emotional speeches. Before heading up the hill toward town, he paused and took one fatherly look at me.

"Mua wama," he said. We will be back.

I have seen friendly relations between American dads and their sons, but my father and I were not buddies; we were father and son.

Doris and I spent the day quietly. We expected everyone to return by bedtime. Doris cooked our meal as usual and reserved some for the absent men. It was getting dark, so Doris gave me a cold bath, even though my mother had warned my father not to allow me to wash with cold water. A doctor had told her that cold baths were not advisable until I grew into a teenager. It had something to do with my premature birth, pneumonia, and rheumatism.

We were barely settled in bed when we heard a loud bang on the door followed by heavy sounds as rebels jumped out of their truck to surround our house. I thought my father had come home, but the story was a different one when Doris opened the door. The rebels rushed into the house screaming and pounding on everything in their way. When they were satisfied with their haphazard search, they shoved us into the back of an old military truck. It was terrifying, but I hated giving anyone the satisfaction of seeing me cry, so I held my breath and refused to shed a tear.

There were many of us in the truck, but we could not see each other through the darkness. The truck was filled with a suffocating stench that indicated the presence of rebels all around us. A cough or two revealed the presence of other civilians. No one said anything as we drove through familiar quarters of Voinjama. We drove past Multilateral High School, where my father was a tutor, and entered a part of the town I had never seen before, heading toward a narrow track of road that ran through a wooded area and up the hill toward a checkpoint. We had left Voinjama behind.

I got anxious. I moved closer to somebody I thought was Doris. I was holding onto another person, and that's what mattered at the time. I was unafraid of dying, because like most children, I did not know death. Children are more daring because they do not have the same awareness of death's finality that adults do. Most children are afraid of things they perceive could render them physical harm. As soon as the threat of physical danger disappeared, I became calm and my mind wandered to curious explorations of what was ahead for us. The rebels at the checkpoint lowered the rope, and the truck drove to an open area in front of a large rectangular building. It was dark, but the truck's headlights illuminated the building, which was divided into two sections by a center parlor. The rebels ordered us out of the truck and told us to stand in line at the entrance of the building. No one was harmed, except for the pushing and yelling. The rebels were more interested in finishing the mission and returning to their usual night of taking drugs.

The adult males were stripped naked and told to enter the gate on the right. I could hear rustling and clanking as the men unbuttoned their shirts and unbuckled their belts. They were pushed into cells behind metal doors. There were two or more cells in each section of the building. I was shoved into one of the cells on the left with Doris and another woman who was carrying a baby and a toddler. Every now and then the baby made one of those sounds that under normal circumstances would have invited even strangers to engage in baby talk. Our cell was dark and bare, occupied only by the lingering ghosts of past detainees. We had brought nothing, so we had nothing to spread over ourselves or to cover the floor. I leaned against a wall and unwillingly surrendered myself to the floor. But as nauseating as our cell was, it was not the reason I didn't fall asleep that first night.

In the impenetrable darkness, I noticed that we were not alone. I heard groans of such acute pain that I could feel the intensity of the invisible victim's suffering. It sounded as though he had already surrendered in spirit, and the groans were the involuntary lamentations the body makes on behalf of the soul when all strength is gone. I could not fall asleep no matter how hard I tried. Outside, crickets kept their own vigil, interrupted only by the regularity of the groans, which had become a rhythmic undertone to the trilling chants of loud-mouth insects outside our cell. I pushed myself against the wall as if to blend in to the cold cement barrier, but I remained in place, and it seemed that time froze until dawn.

It was about the time of morning when under normal, peaceful circumstances one hears the voice of an imam chanting or the beating of a *tabi*, a drum used to call morning prayers. Even non-Muslims in many African cities appreciate the punctual voice of a local imam chanting the classic prayers that serve as a community wake-up call. For the first time since the war started, I missed the melodic voice from our local mosque. Nor could I any longer hear the groans of our cellmate as the invading sun changed from yellow to blinding white. The man's soul had departed, and his body was no longer obliged to produce the dutiful sounds that had kept him holding on. A few minutes before the cocks would have stopped crowing, had the rebels not eaten them all, the rebels came and took his body away. Two men picked him up by his hands and feet as though he were a heavy sack. I could see Doris in her corner directly opposite me. There was nothing to talk about. What could we have discussed? We remained in our separate places until the rebels ordered us out for air.

The men, still locked in their cells, were having their morning devotion. Many of the detained Sierra Leoneans, Ghanaians, and Nigerians were Catholics, and the rebels allowed them to sing and pray. From the very first day of our arrest until the day we walked out of prison, the adults started and ended their day with hymns and prayers. They sometimes sang a song we used to sing before communion, when the priest whispered prayers and quietly assigned tasks to altar boys before inviting congregants to partake in the Eucharist:

> All to Jesus I surrender;
> humbly at his feet I bow.
> Worldly pleasures all forsaken;
> take me, Jesus, take me now.

At the time, all I heard was a song, but I now imagine the feelings of those men as they surrendered themselves to their only remaining hope, God. There were no worldly pleasures to be forsaken, and what the prisoners were telling God was that they stood literally naked in supplication. They wanted to be filled with God's love and power to endure the horrors of their imprisonment.

A few days after we arrived at the prison, the men were allowed outside, and I got to see my father, Patrick, and Mr. Jamiru. I was happy to see that they had not completely lost their spirits. Patrick cracked jokes about the horrific experiences they had been through, and my father was his usual wise self. They had been harassed and humiliated by children who should have been in their classrooms, but they were unbroken. In that brief moment nothing seemed to have changed, and we were together like we had been on the Sundays before we were prisoners. Everyone laughed when Patrick called me Small Prisoner. I was reassured by the fact that the men found humor in our situation. After a while, they were ordered to return to their cells, but the women and children were allowed to stay outside longer. The rebels were not concerned with me or the women. They often let me roam freely around the prison. I sometimes wandered into nearby farms to dig remnant potatoes or cassava.

We were not political prisoners or prisoners of conscience. Instead, we were what I call war prisoners: civilians arbitrarily detained in a war. Although Charles Taylor issued the order that led to our arrest, our fate lay directly in the hands of the rebels around us. They could decide whether we lived or died. When I later became an Amnesty International organizer at my high school in Norway and was responsible for coordinating student letters to presidents and prime ministers on behalf of political prisoners and prisoners of conscience, I sometimes wondered whether anyone had known about me when I was a prisoner. In those days, we listened to BBC and heard about famous political prisoners like Nelson Mandela of South Africa's African National Congress (ANC) and African rebel leaders such as John Garang of the Sudan People's Liberation Army (SPLA) and Jonas Savimbi of the National Union for the Total Liberation of Angola (UNITA), but never about us. Although the battle over Monrovia was always on the news, we were what Taylor liked to call the grass in the clash of elephants—we suffered.

Because the rebels were acting on their own discretion, their actions toward prisoners needed no justification and they were answerable to no one. Some days, they raised the security alert to maximum without any particular change in circumstances at the prison or in Voinjama. We were not allowed outside on those days. The men were stripped and subjected to hours of nakedness. I was sometimes allowed to take things to my father, Mr. Jamiru, or Patrick in the adult cells, but I refused to enter the cells when the men had their clothes confiscated. I abhorred the attempt to humiliate and kill the spirit of my father and his colleagues by subjecting them to the indignity of forced nakedness. I protested by not going anywhere near the male cells on days when I might have seen my father and his colleagues, some of whom had been teachers at my school, naked.

There was little opportunity to illegally obtain anything in prison, especially because there was nothing left of the country, but somehow cigarettes, pens, paper, and other contraband occasionally found their way into the cells. I was often responsible for transporting contraband between prisoners and conniving visitors. I learned how to clandestinely transport fire into the cells so the prisoners could smoke their smuggled cigarettes. I could contain a small ember in the palm of my hand by swinging my arm fast and running toward the cells. The rebels assumed I was playing around and failed to notice that I was carrying a glowing coal. I became such an expert fire smuggler that I was never caught, and the rebels only found out that the prisoners had been smoking by the stale smell of cigarettes in the cells. Every successful delivery brought joy to the desolate faces of the prisoners. It was satisfying to know that the adults depended on me for a mission that brought a little light to the darkness of their imprisonment. When one is confined and deprived of everything, even bad habits can become good consolations.

Life as a war prisoner became routine after a while. The adults sang their hymns and said their prayers, and I spent my day in the prison yard with the women, doing nothing. The adults were allowed a few minutes outside, the rebels played with their AK-47s, and every now and then a familiar visitor brought us food. Mandela was right when he said that "routine is the supreme law of prison in almost every country of the world, and every day is for all practical purposes like the day before: the same surroundings, same faces, same dialogue, same odor, walls rising to the skies, and the ever-present feeling that outside the prison gates there is an exciting world to which you have no access." Although our prison situation, I believe, was worse than conditions on Robben Island as related by Mandela, the underlying idea was the same. Soon enough we knew what made each of our captors click and what to expect on most days. For instance, whenever a plane flew above the prison, the rebels let loose a fusillade into the sky until they were satisfied that the plane, usually a random commercial aircraft, was completely out of sight.

Then there was the regular torture of Old Man Zazay. Zazay was a retired member of the Armed Forces of Liberia. He was the kind of haggard retiree one finds in most African military barracks: an aged man who has devoted his entire life to the military, and for whom retirement means surrendering to an inglorious death. They are given shanty quarters and enough supplies to keep them busy. Zazay's love for taking care of weapons kept him in the barracks even though he was well over retirement age. The rebels wanted to know what he knew about President Doe and where his comrades hid their weapons. They would drag him out of his cell and kick him and beat him with gun butts while interrogating him. Some mornings, he could barely walk on his own. Sometimes he responded in Liberian English: "Ar nar know nartin, ma children"—I know nothing, my children. Other times, he just lay there as they trampled on his wrinkled body with their boots and rifles. It bothered me the first time, and then torture, too, became normalized, and witnessing the pain of others no longer troubled me.

The rebels sometimes drove away with a prisoner who never returned. One day, Old Man Zazay was driven away. The only prisoner who was officially released without being driven away was a Sierra Leonean man by the name of Momoh. I recall his release because my father and his friends gave me a piece of paper that I smuggled out of their cell and delivered to him before he departed. It was, I later found out, a secret note informing President Momoh about plans to invade Sierra Leone. I remember Momoh as a loud man who was not afraid of the rebels. He must have had a strong connection to the NPFL that guaranteed his freedom almost as soon as he was imprisoned.

One morning, our captors told us they had been ordered to release some prisoners. We unceremoniously walked out of prison in 1991. Voinjama was not even a shell of its vivacious old self. It had gone from a city to something resembling an abandoned graveyard. The few remaining inhabitants walked around in the shadows of their diminished bodies like sufferers of terminal diseases who had already surrendered to imminent death. Many rebels had forgotten about the war and were only surviving by the illusive power of their rusty weapons. The drugs that previously had transformed them into young monsters were no longer forthcoming, and many were forced to succumb to the torment of a sober conscience. There were those who joined the NPFL believing that the war would comprise just a few surgical fights, after which everything would return to normal, but even though violent confrontations had ceased in most parts of Liberia, the war was not yet over. We remained in Voinjama for a few weeks while my father planned our return to Sierra Leone. Patrick, Mr. Jamiru, and Doris decided to stay in Voinjama.

There are many things I still do not understand because my father chose not to share the full meaning of some events. He may have omitted details of certain occurrences in order to spare my young mind from the complex burden of full knowledge of the horrors that surrounded us. He did his best to make life seem normal even when reality on the ground needed no interpretation. Only so much is concealable about the blatant torture of innocent civilians by child soldiers young enough to be their offspring, or about the fact that one had to go through a security gate constructed of human skeletons to enter the prison yard. Even without the rebels constantly threatening everyone with the warning "If you *fuckor*"—fuck up—"you will die," I knew the chances of survival were narrow, perhaps even impossible.

I never understood what fucking up would entail, but I hoped each day throughout the war that death would never come my way, especially after witnessing some of the torture, and the manner in which dead bodies were buried just deep enough for vultures to uncover the corpses. Burial was not a part of the killing ritual, except to reduce the pungent smell of human remains that often suffocated all of us, rebel and civilian. People were frequently shot on bridges so their corpses would fall into the river. No one dared to *fuckor* after witnessing one of those public executions, unless they wanted to be escorted. *Escort* euphemistically referred to the journey between a victim's arrest and the riverbank or roadside where he or she was put to death. The rebels believed that by killing their victim, they were making his or her journey from the world to heaven shorter, or simply fulfilling the Liberian and Sierra Leonean courtesy of walking with one's visitor for some of his or her return journey, carrying on unfinished conversations and sending messages to those whom the visitor was returning to. But how one could *fuckor* was simply a matter of luck. It could range from laughing too hard at a commander's joke to looking "ugly." When a commander declared, "Dae mordor fuckor deng ugly"—the motherfucker is damn ugly— the poor target of his observation might be escorted for the crime of not being handsome. Killings like this have made it impossible to place the Liberian and Sierra Leonean civil wars into ideological context. They were revolutions fought by lunatics who thought their biggest enemies were those with a peculiar sense of humor, or the subjectively hideous ones.

But when I was in prison, the rebels were very fond of me and enjoyed making fun of me. They would tell me their secret missions and things they had heard from Charles Taylor—Ganghay or Papay, as he was known among his warriors. From the rebels I found out that the war was about to extend to Sierra Leone, and that some of the rebels manning our prison were already signed up to fight for Corporal Foday Sankoh, leader of the Revolutionary United Front (RUF) of Sierra Leone. But it was folly to believe everything that came out of the mouths of intoxicated and bloodthirsty child soldiers, youths who admired my father for his education but would not hesitate to torture him. The duty of a child soldier, in essence, was to be "brave, strong, and intelligent" and to execute their "duty before complaint." In other words, they had to kill their victim before questioning the motive behind his death, if they ever did. A soldier who questioned orders was a *gbelleh soja*, a sissy who must be escorted, too.

I used to view child soldiers as vandals and heartless killers, but now I know that we were all victims of the same circumstances.

Rebel and civilian, we were always praying for freedom or God's protection. It is like the prayers of a beast and its prey. God must either be amused or baffled by their devotion. The beast sees the animal of prey and says, "Thank you, God, for granting me this day my daily bread," and the animal of prey cries out to God for speed in order to escape the beast chasing it. The wars in Liberia and Sierra Leone produced a system in which one was to either kill or be killed. This was the reality in that region for more than a decade.

For commanders like Charles Taylor of the NPFL and Foday Sankoh of the RUF, war was about power and control of the wheel of government. But for most child soldiers, it was mainly a survival mechanism. They had been victims before they became victimizers. When children were conscripted to become child soldiers, they were drugged, tortured, and put to a test of loyalty by being ordered to kill their first victims. Sometimes it was somebody they had known for a long time, a relative or a friend. In extreme cases, they were ordered to eat the heart and drink the blood of their first victims in order to become members of what was known in Liberia as SBU, Small Boys Unit. Members of this unit would offer you a joint and shoot you in the head later. But I remained invincible to them, or maybe according to doctrinal execution I was not ugly enough to warrant death at the time.

Apart from long sermons or songs about how the AK-47 assault rifle was their father and mother, or the less frequent requests for me to carry out some sort of prison chore, or attempts to scare me from misbehaving, the rebels were never interested in my movements around the prison yard. Perhaps they were aware that I would never consider escaping and leaving my father in prison. If I had, I might have ended up like them, trapped in the vicious cycle of war and death.

As time progressed in prison, I became more aware of my predicament and the possibility of dying in jail. I would go to bed on the empty floor of my cell and think of my brothers and sisters in Sierra

Leone, and what food my mother might be preparing at home. I could imagine the cooking aromas of potato leaves, cassava leaves, and peanut butter soup. Sometimes, just when I was about to think of whether we would make it home for Christmas, I would hear the other prisoners sing one of our morning songs:

> What kind of man is Jesus, alleluia
> He made the sun to shine, alleluia
> He made the blind to see, alleluia
> He made the deaf to hear, alleluia

Every time I wake up in some peaceful corner of the United States, it feels like I've risen from a long nightmare and found myself in paradise, a place completely different from my prison cell on the outskirts of Voinjama, where I woke up to the chronic smell of urine, feces, and decayed bodily fluids. A Christian would say that God has a habit of subjecting his humble servants to rigid tests, but what about the God of my grandmother, whom she worshipped five times a day? What about the incantations that my elders offered to our ancestors? What about my own endurance, diligence, and perseverance? Was God awake with me in my moments of fear, or was he hibernating even as evil prevailed among his children? But what God goes to sleep while his creation self-destructs? Unless, of course, there is no God, and man is, as Jean-Paul Sartre asserted, condemned to be free. Many unanswered questions remain about those years of calamity in Liberia and Sierra Leone, but God is not on trial; it is man who must answer for his own deeds.

CHAPTER 2

There will be times when it is not the answer
but the question itself that determines the path.

May 27, 2004, was an ordinary day in Oslo, but unlike many other days in Norway, it seemed like the sun might shine, or at least it seemed quite unlikely that rain would fall. I had been waiting in front of the U.S. embassy all morning with my friends Erik and Andreas, and we had been teasing and laughing at each other. But as it got closer to eight a.m., the hour I had been waiting for since I'd been accepted to Skidmore College a few months prior, no one dared say a word, not even the jovial Erik. Erik Bolmstrand, a Swedish classmate from Red Cross Nordic United World College (RCNUWC), the high school I had just graduated from, was with me because we had plans to travel together to his home in Sweden after my U.S. visa was processed. Andreas is a friend I worked with as a guest speaker on Sierra Leone for the Norwegian student solidarity movement Operation Day's Work (ODW).

The idea of ODW had been adopted in Norway when a young member of the Norwegian Student Union challenged the 1964 annual meeting of that organization to extend its campaign for improved conditions in schools to less fortunate parts of the world. He argued that it was wrong to focus merely on Norway's own schools when so many young people in other parts of the world had no opportunity to go to school. This action by Norwegian students, in my view, captures the essence of the Christian teaching of being our brother's keeper. Today, ODW raises thirty million kroner annually to provide educational opportunities around the world. In 2002, the organization was procuring funds for educational reconstruction in Sierra Leone, and I spent some parts of my first semester in Norway visiting various participating high schools, including RCNUWC, to talk about Sierra Leone and the importance of rebuilding the country's educational infrastructure after the civil war. It was the beginning of a life devoted to advocating for education and African development.

The U.S. embassy represented a crossroads between two worlds that were to determine my future. Either I would go back to Sierra Leone with an International Baccalaureate (IB) diploma and continue the struggle in a country still recovering from a decade of war, or I would obtain a visa and pursue further education in the United States. I was no longer willing to consider the former option, because life in Sierra Leone would never be the same for a Just Comes (JC), the local title for those who return from the West. A JC is no longer a member of his own community; he is considered to have evolved to the imagined status of Western affluence. No one is expected to return, not permanently at least, after successfully waving good-bye to the land of his birth in West Africa. I say "successfully" because it is indeed considered a great success when one survives the rigorous scrutiny of consular officers and obtains a visa to live in a Western country. The expectation is that the person assumes the responsibility of taking care of his family at home. This is why many Africans feel obliged to stay in the West in spite of despicable hardship and would do anything to get there.

It is difficult to be selfish when an entire extended family relies on one for its survival. This type of social arrangement has always been a valuable part of most African societies. An African does not live in isolation from his neighbor. Those with more in the community are expected to share with those who have less. Archbishop Tutu has described this interconnectivity of human existence as a "bundle of life" in which we are governed by the African concept of *ubuntu*: "You are generous, you are hospitable, you are friendly and caring and compassionate. You share what you have. It is easy to say, 'My humanity is caught up, is inextricably bound up, in yours.'" A community that is wrapped in the "bundle of life" shares its resources. When I was a child, one could visit a random Sierra Leonean town and receive room and board from any resident. Sometimes people offered their own beds to complete strangers. Neighbors returned from their farms with food for their less fortunate neighbors. When my mother noticed that a neighbor's kitchen was cold, which meant they had done no cooking that day, she would offer a bowl of food from our kitchen. Whenever we were ready to eat a meal, my mother would shout out to all who were near, "Una mek we eat o," which was a general invitation to all within earshot that they were welcome to partake in our meal. We never ate a meal without this ritualistic invitation to our neighbors.

Unfortunately, African societies are becoming pathetically individualistic, and one of our only hopes for success has become a voyage to the West. Many young Africans are willing to take extreme measures to flee their homes for a promise of hope overseas. Some even risk their lives by crossing the Mediterranean from North Africa in makeshift canoes, but others, like me, will simply get there when we can. I was not brave enough to join the voyage from North Africa to Lampedusa. I have always put my faith in the recompense of merit and in doing what is in my capacity to do in order to get where I want to be. I learned in Sunday school that "he who does not enter the sheep pen by the gate but climbs in by some other means is a thief and a robber. But he who enters by the door is the Shepherd of the sheep. To him the gatekeeper opens the door" (John 10:1–3). Maybe John would think otherwise if he witnessed the kinds of human misery that compel people to abandon their homes and march through hell for even a minuscule promise of hope elsewhere. After two years of successful IB studies in Norway and a prestigious scholarship to study in the United States, I was obsessed by the need to set foot in America, the perceived Promised Land for many Africans.

I was extremely happy to have made it as far as Norway, but I was also haunted by the fear that a failure at this stage would turn into an embarrassing stigma at home. Many West Africans consider it absurd for an individual to travel all the way to Europe and return with a mere high school diploma, without any money to feed his family. One becomes an object of ridicule to those who have never even tried to stay in school, and that was what scared me: the shameful prospect of returning home as a JC without European wealth in my pocket. Education is great and prestigious, but money matters. That is really why we invest in school. Even a philosopher king must eat! The American civil rights leader Dr. Martin Luther King Jr. wrote, "At rock bottom we are neither poets, athletes, nor artists; our existence is centered in the fact that we are consumers, because we first must eat and have shelter to live." I had attained the IB, but I was not yet adequately prepared to embark on a meaningful realization of my dream of assisting in the rebuilding of my war-ravaged country. If I was to make an impact on the lives of my fellow Sierra Leoneans, I needed an education superior to a high school diploma.

Even though the United States, or what most Sierra Leoneans refer to as Amaika, had never been a dream for me, I was elated by the genuineness of the documents I had been carrying for more than two months like a baby kangaroo in its mother's pouch. As I stood in front of the embassy, I was haunted by a sinister anxiety. But there was no reason for me to be nervous, or so I thought. I was about to travel to the United States, and my friends were standing at the embassy with me. My Sierra Leonean elders have a saying that a chick underneath its mother's wings should not be afraid of flying eagles. But like a chick that had survived an unfortunate encounter with the beak of an eagle, I could never be sure of my safety, even under the watchful eyes of the embassy guards.

"Good morning, ladies and gentlemen, welcome to the embassy of the United States of America in Oslo. To begin this morning's procedure, all U.S. citizens move to one side, and the rest of you stay where you are." The command came from one of the guards. Another was vigilantly watching over his shoulders. Snipers stood sentry all over the roof of the four-story triangular embassy block facing Henrik Ibsen Street. A temporary wire fence had been constructed as a barrier between the building and the street. Erik and Andreas had to find somewhere to wait, because the embassy did not tolerate "loitering." Terrorist threats to U.S. properties around the world had increased since September 11, 2001, and again since the declaration of war on Iraq in 2003. Everything and every person going into and out of the embassy was subject to stringent inspection. Even embassy workers who seemed to have known each other for a long time were subject to security measures, although for them it occurred under a less intense atmosphere of *Hello, how are you, how was your night?*

Erik and Andreas left for a nearby café to wait for me. The instant the guard separated the foreigners from the U.S. citizens, I began to feel the solitude of standing alone in a crowd. The implied preferential treatment made me conscious of my own citizenship: I was a Sierra Leonean standing on U.S. territory in Norway. I had been separated from my best friends. I felt empty. Was it loneliness or fear? I was not sure, but I was shivering and sweating, obvious signs of nervousness. I had traveled all night on a bus from Flekke to Oslo with my classmates. I was still filled with the emotions of saying good-bye to friends with whom I had spent the last two years at RCNUWC. I had not had anything to eat that morning, but I was usually all right going for long hours without food. Whatever the reason for my nervousness, I had to stride with strength and hope. I knew that deep down, the rod and staff of my savior would comfort my weary soul and help me survive the morning. Or perhaps Mahin Gewor, the god of my ancestors, would lead my way through the embassy gate.

One of the guards instructed me to place my bag on the scanner and empty my pockets. His voice no longer scared me, as it had when he'd instructed us to stand in separate lines. I was not intimidated because I had heard his voice before, or maybe my stubbornness made me disregard shows of power. I detest unnecessary assertion of authority when the point can be made without such farce. The alarm went off as I walked through the screening machine. A guard pulled me to the side of the line to conduct a physical search. The X-ray baton moved up and down my impassive body. I tried to avoid eye contact with the guard, but I couldn't fail to notice that he sounded like Vijay, one of the American students at RCNUWC. I had studied philosophy with Vijay, and he was the only student whose accent I never failed to identify among the array of RCNUWC nationals speaking other dialects of English.

I was told to leave my possessions at the gate and pick them up on my way out to avoid further searches. A young lady led me to the reception desk.

"Where in the States are you going?" she asked.

"New York," I responded with a smile.

"Wow, family? Friends?" she asked again.

"*Nie*," I replied in a playful Norwegian dialect that hadn't left my tongue since I was taught how to say no. "College," I stressed, to make an impression.

"Good for you!" she said.

We arrived at the entrance to the embassy building reserved for consular visits. She left me at the door and disappeared behind a wooden cubicle. During our brief conversation, she seemed to be the only human being among the human robots I'd encountered at the embassy. Even between the devil and the deep blue sea, there can be a breath of fresh air. I was anxious to know what was beyond the cubicle. The entire atmosphere began to feel like what Mende people refer to as the passing of a *genei*, a spirit. I got goose bumps from the motionless quiet and chill of the corridor.

Most of what I know about being Mende, my father's ethnic group, I learned from my grandmother Mama Jeneba, my father's mother. When I was born prematurely, in the sixth or seventh month (depending on which relative narrates my nativity story), my mother did not know what to do, so she entrusted me to my grandmother, who was considered an expert at herbal medicine. To save my life, my grandmother visited every herbalist she could find. She would wrap me in her improvised incubator of multiple blankets and place me in a circle of kerosene lamps. She fed me with finger droplets of warm water until I was strong enough to eat normal baby food. I knew no other parental figure throughout my early childhood. That is why when I was first asked to state my name for my kindergarten teachers, I said, "I am Joe Jeneba." I believed up to the point when I started living with my father in Liberia that my grandmother was my sole parent. She took me to Friday prayers at the local mosque, bought my toys, protected me from harm, and shared her cozy bed with me until I left Sierra Leone to live with my father in Liberia. Family legend has it that she had started saving money for my college education even before I could pronounce my first words. She had offered proceeds from her sales of bananas, tobacco, cacao, coffee, and oranges to my father for safekeeping, but he jokingly rejected the money, saying he could afford to educate his own children. I am the de facto heir to her coffee, cacao, and orange plantations in Sami and Geima, two villages a few miles outside Pendembu. Several years have passed since I last set eyes on my inheritance, but I always carry my grandmother with me. She is my inspiration and the source of my strength.

Life with my grandmother brought me closer to the geneis of our culture. There are good and evil geneis, and a person had to smear on his body various kinds of *nesie*, potions made out of herbs and blessed with Koranic verses, in the morning or at night to avoid the spells of the evil ones. My grandmother made it her duty to bathe me regularly in one of her several bottles of nesie or to cleanse me with steam from boiling herbs to cure diseases. I was not a big fan of the herbal-medicine body-cleansing process. Herbs are boiled in a large pot for several hours, and the sick person together with the boiled herbs is placed under several blankets while the cover of the pot is gradually removed to diffuse the steam under the blanket. It is literally a sauna under a blanket. If the right herbs are used, it is believed to be a great cure for diseases such as jaundice, malaria, or yellow fever—all of which regularly attacked me when I was a child. My grandmother also made me drink a particularly nasty antimalaria herb called *gbangba*. One could taste its bitterness hours after consumption.

It was hard to determine whether my grandmother's herbs worked, since my mother always took me to the hospital for further treatment. My parents allowed my grandmother to do whatever she wanted with me, as a compromise for them to do whatever they deemed necessary for me without her protestation. Mama Jeneba was allowed to give me her herbal medicines, as long as my parents reserved the right to a second medical opinion. I followed Mama Jeneba to prayers at the mosque, as long as it did not interfere with Sunday school. I loved the steam from the pot, but I could not stand the smell or taste of the bush herbs. Coincidentally, my love for heat turned out to be a good preparation for my sauna days in Scandinavia. Going to a sauna has become one of my preferred recreational activities.

My grandmother never tolerated chance when it came to matters concerning my life. She even believed that my premature birth was an attempt by some jealous evildoer to kill me in order to deny her a grandson, something she had wished for since my older sister Hawa was born, and as far as she was concerned, if another attempt on my life occurred, the malfeasant had to die. We were almost always together when I was not in school or playing with other kids, and we became known throughout Pendembu as Mama Jeneba and her "husband." Family members referred to me as her bodyguard, but I believe she was the guard, not me. Only in the company of my grandmother was I assured of complete safety from my father's whip or the meanness of other children. However, my grandmother's love for me also placed me out of favor with my competitive siblings and relatives. One such relative was my cousin Sisi Jeneba, my grandmother's namesake, who always competed for my grandmother's attention. Her stern competition often left me crying, either from her endless teasing or because she deliberately ate whatever food my grandmother had reserved for me. Sisi Jeneba resided in Kenema and only visited during major holidays, but her visits always disrupted my life with my grandmother. My older sister Hawa lived with Sisi Jeneba and her family in Kenema.

Mama Jeneba accompanied me to every appointment and many school events that required the presence of a parent. But there I was years later, standing in the U.S. Embassy in Oslo by myself. In the cubicle before me, which seemed like a temporary addition to the interior of the building to facilitate the further vetting of visitors, a young man sat behind a window. I stubbed my right foot at the door, which caused me to conclude that whatever was behind the wall was not in my favor. As a child, I noticed that whenever I was on my way to visit relatives, stubbing my right foot meant they were not home. I am always unlucky when I stub my right foot. It was my grandmother who first called my attention to this unique phenomenon. She had explanations for the unusual things that no one else could understand. The rapid trembling of my eyelids or the random appearance of a bug in a place where it shouldn't be means a visitor should be expected. I never worry about a swollen left eye because I still believe that it is a premonition of something good. She was often right: the hosts were never home, the visitors came, and fortune always compensated my swollen eye. But I wondered whether to trust the communication with my feet so many years after my grandmother's death.

Inside the embassy, I was disappointed to see only a huge room with cubicles. In the middle of the room was the reception area, with the U.S. flag standing sadly in the corner. I know the flag carries great pride for Americans, but not in that quiet parlor of the embassy in Oslo. It was confined to a corner and received no salutes or admiration, only the gaze of anxious visa applicants casting their lots for a place in the United States, some in pursuit of the American dream, others maybe terrorists. I stared at the flag for a few minutes, almost in sanctimonious homage, but it ignored my gaze like a rebuked child. It stood bashful and folded, like *Mimosa pudica* in response to human touch.

A lady in one of the cubicles instructed me to pay my visa application fee of $100. I do not remember for sure, but I think it was also required that the applicant pay with a single $100 bill. I moved forward and pushed a $100 bill through a pigeonhole. I handed over the rest of my documents through the same hole and returned to my seat. I had been waiting for this day for a long time, but as I sat in front of that indifferent flag, I worried that events might not turn out well. I thought of stubbing my foot on my way into the room and the lengthy background questionnaire I'd filled out a few weeks before. I wished I were confident enough to accept the superstitious signs that I'd had no problem believing when I was a child within the safe haven of my grandmother's watch. But the visa application questionnaire, with its strange yes-or-no answers, had intimidated me, and I didn't know what to expect from the interview. I tried to imagine possible questions and to rehearse my answers, but nothing seemed to make sense to me right then. I was too anxious about the interview. I was also nervous about being alone in that room and knowing that I was being watched by someone in one of the many rooms behind those glass windows. I made a conscious attempt to sit still.

I had never been to the United States, but for some reason the waiting room gave me a feeling of being there already. The decor was different from that of other public spaces I had seen in Norway. Maybe it was the flag or the framed picture of the Capitol in Washington, DC. Those two objects were the most familiar symbols of the United States to me, yet they had never brought so much intimidation, so much fear to my heart. I had always looked upon the United

States as a great country. It was one of the nations that had helped me survive during my life as a refugee in Guinea. Most of the food items from the United Nations High Commissioner for Refugees (UNHCR) were stamped "USA" or adorned with a huge star and a few red and white stripes. This is what the United States had meant to me before I went to Norway. Maybe it was why I found myself falling in love with everything American and supported nearly every form of U.S. foreign policy.

I also had great admiration for Dr. King and his leadership of the American civil rights movement. I had read his "Letter from a Birmingham Jail" in high school and felt inspired by his convictions. I pictured a lowly prisoner sitting in a naked corner of his dingy cell, painfully attempting to defend truths that should have been self-evident, especially to people in his profession—the clergy. The reverend provided for his colleagues one of the best elucidations of the biblical requisite to be our brother's keeper by writing, "Injustice anywhere is a threat to justice everywhere. We are caught in an inescapable network of mutuality, tied in a single garment of destiny. Whatever affects one directly affects all indirectly." Because many in the clergy were concerned with the legality of Dr. King's actions, he endeavored to outline the meaning of just and unjust laws. He explained that just laws are those that are squarely premised on moral law, and unjust laws are those that are out of harmony with moral laws and degrade the human personality. The activist has every right not to abide by unjust laws; but if he chooses to violate them in civil disobedience, he must do so openly in order to effect change.

In my own work with poor people in Sierra Leone, I have come to understand how agonizing it is to be deliberately misunderstood by those who ought to know better. As Dr. King framed it, "Shallow understanding from people of good will is more frustrating than absolute misunderstanding from people of ill will." In Sierra Leone, we say it's easier to awaken a man who is asleep than the one who is merely pretending to sleep. When an individual absolutely misunderstands your position, you can work harder at bringing him to understanding; but when such an individual is merely pretending to misunderstand you, there is nothing you can do to change his mind. It becomes his prerogative to accept or reject your position, and your arguments, whether rational or irrational, cogent or incongruent, become irrelevant. He is the hypocrite of the Bible who refuses to cast out the beam from his own eye so that he can see clearly to remove the mote from his brother's eye. It is repeatedly a defense of inaction by people of goodwill in the face of injustice to feign lack of knowledge in order to hide in the shadow of ignorance.

When I was a child, Sierra Leoneans were captivated by the spectacular performance of Eddie Murphy in the film *Coming to America*. When Michael Jackson did his trademark moonwalk, all the children did their best to become little MJs. We carried postcard-size pictures of him and jumped to our feet whenever one of his songs played on the radio. Bill Clinton was my first mental image of what a president or a statesman should look like. We Sierra Leoneans were not concerned with his impeachment trials, perhaps because marital indiscretions are overlooked aspects of our own patriarchy. I developed a great emotional connection to the Texan griot Don Williams, whom my father loved more than any other musician. I grew up listening to my father whistle Williams songs when the cassette wasn't playing. To remember my father after he died, I listened to Williams' soothing country voice, and he became my favorite singer of all time. Don Williams, like the praise singers of Africa, is a master of folktales and a champion of romance. I can still picture my father on Sunday mornings when he walked around the house singing along to Williams' "I Recall a Gypsy Woman."

When it came to images of strength, valor, and brotherhood, I looked to the U.S. military. Even today I am moved by the recruitment commercials of the U.S. Marine Corps. The dragging of the bodies of U.S. soldiers and Marines in the streets of Mogadishu during the 1993 battle in Somalia angered me. It was not the killing of the soldiers that bothered me most; in fact, more Somalis died that day. It was the desecration of dead bodies that raised my outrage. Trampling on the corpses of even our enemies only makes us into savages. I also took it personally when American embassies in Kenya and Tanzania were bombed in 1998, leaving hundreds of Africans dead. I remember particularly having great admiration for the United States during the noncombatant emergency evacuation of Americans and Europeans from Freetown in May 2000 by British paratroopers and the U.S. Navy. Many Sierra Leoneans watched hopelessly as Americans and Europeans lined up at the Mammy Yoko helipad to be flown home. I sat in the window of the second floor in my uncle's étage (two-story building) on the edge of the sea in Murray Town to admire the majestic flights of double-propeller Chinook and Lynx helicopters between Mammy Yoko and Lungi International Airport.

The American and European population in Freetown was not very large, especially after almost nine years of civil war, but a great nation cares for even the smallest number of its citizens abroad. That display of U.S. military might and governmental responsibility was very impressive. The soldiers were not in Sierra Leone to participate in the war; they were there on the order of their commander in chief to bring their compatriots home and to assist with the deployment of UN peacekeepers. During those days of despair for every Sierra Leonean, I was fascinated by the United States of America—a country I had never known, a place far beyond the vast ocean spread across the view from my window. I remember wanting to become American so that I could fly away to a country where I could go to bed and wake up in peace. But none of that would prove helpful in the embassy, especially not the dream of wanting to become an American. I knew that if I wanted a nonimmigrant student visa to the United States, I could not mention any desire to immigrate.

CHAPTER 3

Never allow another person's beef with the
devil to eclipse your accord with God.

As I sat in the embassy reception area waiting for my interview and contemplating my future, I tried to keep my composure. I attempted to convince myself that it was only a visa interview. I had endured enough of life's tribulations to get to the point where I was already the recipient of a prestigious scholarship to study in the United States. A visa interview was just one more hurdle to overcome. One does not quit a race near the finish line. When the journey gets tough, it is always important to remember why one is on the road in the first place. My presence in Norway was evidence of my resilience, a testament to my determination to make a way through the thickest of obstacles and to keep going forward despite the odds. I had one chance at the embassy, and I had to get it right. Sierra Leoneans believe that everything has its place, its standing, its position in the interconnectivity of existence. In the territory of monkeys, each monkey jumps for itself; in the kingdom of fish, fish eats fish; in a flock of birds, each bird snatches what it can. In a gathering of dogs, the modus operandi is "you fall for me, I fall for you." The human criterion is give and take. I was ready to give what was required of me to get what I wanted and proceed to where I desired to be. Despite the natural fear of uncertainty that consumes the human heart in dire circumstances, I was calmed by my determination to go to the United States.

I also had to prepare for the difficult task of engaging in a conversation with a woman. I used to be intimidated by women, although my time at both the Sierra Leone Grammar School (SLGS) and RCNUWC, where I had a few classes with female teachers, lessened my fear of speaking to women. One of the teachers I had at SLGS, Mrs. Nichols, was like a grandmother to her pupils. There was another female teacher at SLGS whom we all feared very much. She had made a student wash his mouth out with scented soap for using profanities in class. But no matter my fear, I needed a visa to the United States, and I had to do whatever was within my power to make that possible. A man with a set goal must simply stick to his plan. I never allow another person's beef with the devil to eclipse my accord with God. In my relations with others, I always make it a goal to offer the best of my abilities so that in the end I have given my all. I am prepared to live with any outcome as long as I am satisfied that I did my best and there was nothing else I could have done.

But it wasn't that simple. The visa application form noted that "a visa may not be issued to persons who are within specific categories defined by law as inadmissible to the United States." The trouble lay in not knowing what categories of people were defined by law as personae non gratae. Another problematic area was the absurdity of some of the questions on the application form. One question, for instance, has a sentence about Nazi persecutions and another about export control violations. Yes or no, "Do you seek to enter the United States to engage in export control violations, subversive or terrorist activities, or any other unlawful purpose? Are you a member or representative of a terrorist organization as currently designated by the U.S. Secretary of State? Have you ever participated in persecutions directed by the Nazi government of Germany; or have you ever participated in genocide?" Of course, an individual may have participated in persecutions directed by the Nazi government of Germany or participated in genocide, but may not be entering the United States to engage in export control violations, subversive or terrorist activities, or for any other unlawful purpose. I simply checked "no."

I also thought she might ask whether I had been directly involved in the Sierra Leonean conflict. It is a question I have had to answer ever since I left Sierra Leone at the end of the war. A friend once blurted out in the middle of an unrelated conversation: "Joseph, did you ever kill anyone . . . like during the war and stuff?" "No," I said. Our mutual friends expected me to be offended by the bluntness of her question, but I saw no ill will in her curiosity. People assume that every child in Sierra Leone or Liberia had engaged in the war as a combatant. The campaign against the use of children in armed conflict inadvertently produced a global presumption that every child who survived the Liberian or Sierra Leonean conflict had been a child soldier. The reason behind the presumption is that the NPFL and RUF had conscripted most children who were old enough to carry a rifle. These children and their commanders raped, tortured, and killed mothers in front of their children; fathers were forced to witness the rape of their women and were afterward tortured to death. Girls were taken as sex slaves, cooks, and porters, while boys were drugged and transformed into killing machines. The drugs temporarily suppressed the children's fears and made them into wanton murderers. As soldiers, they were told they had no need for family other than their comrades in the senseless armed struggle. They were constantly reminded that their rifles were their mothers and fathers. The girls were sometimes given weapons during crucial battles, but their principal role was to satisfy the sexual desires of commanders. As the Liberian conflict became a protracted civil war, various factions created women's units.

I was never a child soldier, but I was a warrior in a struggle to survive the two civil wars. I became an invincible soldier constantly fighting to live for another day. I was also lucky never to be totally separated from my parents throughout the civil wars in both Liberia and Sierra Leone. Whenever the guns were silent and the rebels moderated their violence, my parents were out in search of food. Sometimes they returned with a few cups of rice, a bundle of cassava, or a bag of potatoes. Finding the food was often easier than successfully taking it home to one's family. The rebels waited for people to obtain food, and then they took it away. When we were in prison the adults adhered to the tradition of leaving a few handfuls of food for a child. It is considered heartless in Sierra Leone, Guinea, and Liberia to eat a meal with a child present and leave nothing for the child. Whether one is the parent or not, one does not eat in the presence of a hungry child without sharing the meal. A sacrifice made for a child is considered the greatest among my people.

In law school, I read a nineteenth-century English admiralty case involving three men who killed and ate a lad in order to survive when their vessel, the *Mignonette*, drifted during a stormy sea that left them stranded on a lifeboat with no food. I thought of the fact that all the adults who were imprisoned with me would have rather died to save my life than kill me to preserve their own. In *Regina v. Dudley and Stephens* (1884), the accused persons, Thomas Dudley and Edward Stephens, together with one Edmund Brooks and a teenage orphan by the name of Richard Parker, were caught in a storm on the high seas sixteen hundred miles from the Cape of Good Hope. The four seamen were forced onto an open lifeboat. They had no food or water except for two one-pound tins of turnips. For three days they had nothing else to eat. On the fourth day they caught a small turtle, which they ate for a few days. The turtle was the only food they had for nearly three weeks. The only water they had was the rainwater they collected in their capes.

The boat kept drifting until it was at least a thousand miles from shore. On the twentieth day, Dudley suggested to Stephens and Brooks that they draw a lot to determine who should be eaten to save the rest. Brooks dissented, and young Parker was not consulted on the matter. Dudley and Stephens concluded that since they had families and Parker had no responsibilities, he should be their sacrificial lamb. Parker was already extremely weakened by starvation and consumption of seawater.

Dudley prayed to God for forgiveness and then wedged a knife in Parker's throat, killing him instantly. The three men fed on Parker's body and blood for four days. They were eventually rescued by a passing vessel and charged with murder. The defendants argued that their act had been committed out of necessity. They claimed that their only chance of saving any life was to kill one person for the others to eat. Lord Coleridge held that to preserve one's life is indeed a duty, generally, but it may be the highest duty to sacrifice it. In a similar situation, an average Sierra Leonean man would have sacrificed his life for the child to live. Modernity has brought many changes to our society, and communities are different now, but there was no individualism in the Sierra Leone of my childhood, and the elders protected the young.

"Joseph Kaifala!"

A woman appeared in the center cubicle of the embassy parlor. I quickly raised my head. I was very tired and my heart was pounding. I felt sweat dripping down my chest underneath my shirt. I was thinking of everything and nothing at all. My mind could no longer focus. I was trying to find all possible answers to the dreadful question of what would be my fate if I failed to obtain a visa. I had left a war-ravaged country behind, and ahead of me was an opportunity for a great education.

I stood up slowly and walked to the counter. The woman behind the counter looked at me. I looked back with confidence. There was a sinister air in the exchange. Everything had become so quiet and still. The machines in the back of the room stopped droning, or I stopped hearing them. I was the center of attention. She flipped through my documents once more as if to make sure they were the right papers, or for assurance that she had missed nothing. I became anxious and impatient. The few seconds seemed to last an eternity. Was she going to ask the questions I already knew, the ones about export control violations, subversive or terrorist activities? Was she going to ask any questions at all? I couldn't think of any that were not on the application form.

The woman seemed to have all the time in the world. For her, mine was just another interview, the routine job of an embassy worker. Or perhaps she had never encountered my kind of case in Norway. She was standing between me and my future, but even that did not appear to bother her. She had probably already decided what to tell me at the end of the interview, but she had to conduct the dialogue anyway, as a routine consular procedure. I had paid $100 for the meeting; she was obliged to give me my money's worth.

The delay made me stronger and more resilient. Suddenly I was no longer worried about whether I got the visa or not. In the scheme of things, I had accepted that the outcome of the interview was beyond my control. I wanted to pray, but I stopped myself from doing so. I believe that prayer should be offered as a form of worship or supplication long before I get into trouble. Otherwise God becomes like a fire department that is only called upon when a house is already in flames. God by my understanding should be worshipped even in the most fortunate of times, and he will be there in times of need. This, I believe, is what qualifies God as omnipotent, omniscient, and omnipresent. Muslims pray five times a day in good or bad times. If God is what most religions portray him as, it would be inappropriate to use him merely as an emergency dispatch, a 911 for troubled times.

She started with the minor details, confirming my name and nationality. None of the questions surprised me. Everything proceeds by the book in embassies. But the interview irritated me as much as the application form had. All I needed was a chance to tell the questioner that my future depended on the outcome of our meeting, and that she held the key to the door. I held no illusions that explaining my situation would cause her to bend the rules, but I wanted her to understand that all I hoped for was an opportunity to pursue my education in a country where I had been granted the privilege to do so. She asked a few irrelevant questions that made me believe there was no red flag in my application. After inquiring about how I had gotten to Norway and whether I was a permanent resident, she moved on to what she really wanted to know.

"Why didn't you apply for the visa in your country?"

Apart from the fact that I had been living in Norway for two years, U.S. visas were not issued in my country. There was an American embassy, one of the largest buildings standing in the heart of Freetown, but it did not issue visas. I heard that even the ambassador did not live in Freetown; he traveled between Conakry, Guinea, where he resided, and his office in Freetown. Had U.S. visas been issued in Sierra Leone, I would not have been applying for one in Oslo.

"Is there a neighboring country you can go to?"

"I could go to Liberia, but there is a war going on there," I answered calmly. Most Sierra Leoneans I knew traveled to Senegal for their U.S. visa interviews, but I'd had no money for a trip to Dakar. We came to the end of our inconvenient contact. The glass window stood between us.

"Thank you very much. You may return to your seat." She put her papers in order and returned to the back of the room, that dungeon where my fate would be decided.

I sat down, more anxious than I had been upon first entering the room. I had played my part in the interview; that is, I'd answered questions. I waited for whoever was behind those glass windows to decide my fate. It was then that my worries began. My eyes focused directly on the window, expecting that at any moment someone might emerge. The interval felt like the longest I had had to wait for anything in my life. Yet I had no choice but to wait. My documents were genuine, and I had no criminal record. I had not checked "yes" to being a terrorist or a Nazi genocidaire. A U.S. visa could mean the difference between a decent life and a short life of poverty.

Consular discretion often means that a visa can be denied merely because an official has a doubt, be it substantive or prejudicial. Most African applicants have no means of pursuing a legal recourse for visas denied, so they return home to dead opportunities and shattered dreams.

My brother Francis had told me that not owning a bank account was one of the obstacles that made it impossible for most Sierra Leoneans to travel to the United States. I had immediately opened an account with the Sierra Leone Commercial Bank and deposited about 250,000 Leones—$100. It was not a large sum of money, but it was good enough to convince the consulate that I had an asset in Sierra Leone. The truth is that most Sierra Leoneans would be fortunate to even *visit* a bank, let alone own an account. People who live from hand to mouth do not worry about savings, and most Sierra Leoneans do not know how banks operate. They would not entrust their little wealth, meant for the education of their children, to a stranger in a suit and tie who does not talk straight. They trust, instead, the safety of their *bouyee*, a fanny pack worn underneath the wrapper of most rural women in Sierra Leone.

"Joseph Kaifala!" The woman who had interviewed me called my name.

I rose slowly and stepped to the counter again. The moment, like the seconds just before two bulls lock horns, was intense. She appeared very careful with her words.

"Mr. Kaifala, your visa is denied today under section 214b of the U.S. Immigration and Nationality Act. On this sheet of paper are the descriptions of the criteria for using section 214b. Good luck."

She was unemotional and direct. I reckoned that, unlike me, she had nothing to lose. It was all just another regular work day for a consular officer.

Section 214b describes the consul's discretionary ability to presume immigrant status because the applicant does not demonstrate strong ties to his country of origin, usually based on property or kinship. The relevant section of the act states that "every alien shall be presumed to be an immigrant until he establishes to the satisfaction of the consular officer, at the time of application for a visa, and the immigration officers, at the time of application for admission, that he is entitled to a nonimmigrant status." The law places the burden of proof on the applicant to show that he has strong ties in his country of origin that would compel him to leave the United States at the end of his temporary stay. In my case, the consul was aware that I was not only lucky to be alive, but God only knew how long it would take my country to recover from the devastations of a decade of war. The only demonstrations of strong ties were the papers in my consular file, evidence of academic diligence, and a sense of purpose put together by years of devotion to one cause: a determination to obtain an education.

I inquired about my application fee as I fought back the tears developing under my eyes.

"I'm sorry, visa application fees are nonrefundable," she replied.

If only she'd known how painful it was to give up the money I had saved for months, she would have understood why I gave her such sad face. I had used most of my meager RCNUWC stipend to pay for part of Francis' educational expenses and also for some of the expenses of SAFUGE (Saving the Future Generations), the organization I'd launched in Norway to care for children affected by the war in Sierra Leone. As a scholarship recipient at RCNUWC, I received 1,800 kroner, about $250, annually to spend on minor items not provided by the school. Saving for the $100 visa fee had reduced the share of my stipend I had given to my brother.

I walked out of the embassy building, making a considerable effort to avoid crying. I remembered what my father would have said: "To be a man is not easy, so hold your tears. There are no solutions in tears."

But there are times when even boys must cry. I needed to let my tears roll down my cheeks to pacify my heart. It had been a long morning, and my only comfort was the bright sun shining on Oslo. I looked in its direction; quickly my tears dried away, and I smiled again. I had nothing to give me hope but the brilliance of the morning and the internal echo of one of the songs we had sung during the darkest days of our imprisonment:

> If you believe
> And I believe
> And we together pray,
> The Holy Spirit will come down
> And everything will be safe.

CHAPTER 4

Que será, será.

Erik appeared anxious even before I reached the café where he had been waiting for me. Andreas had left for work. Erik walked hastily toward me for an update. I wanted to handle the moment in a way that would make my friend understand that although events in the embassy had turned out to be such a disappointment, something within made me hopeful rather than sad about the day's outcome. I had overcome my earlier anxiety and was feeling the satisfaction of accomplishment, of the fact that the long-awaited interview was over. I had seen people's lives ruined by a failed U.S. visa interview, and I had quietly harbored worries about my own. I was relieved that it was over, even though my application had been denied. I never let negative emotions subdue the joy of the moment or interfere with the fulfillment of what is in the now. I remembered Jesus' admonishment to his disciples: "So don't worry about tomorrow, for tomorrow will bring its own worries. Today's trouble is enough for today" (Matthew 6:34). My visa troubles were indeed enough for the day. *Inshallah*, God willing, it was not the end of my journey. One failed visa interview, though it altered my plans, could not spell the end of life's promises. Some years before, even if a magic wand had struck me, I could not have imagined attending high school in Norway, but be it by a machination of God or luck, there I was.

My Christian and Muslim upbringing teaches that one should do his utmost best in all circumstances and leave the rest to God. When things go badly I remember a saying of my mother's: *l'homme propose, Dieu dispose*—man proposes, God disposes. We are finite creatures, incapable of perfection. We must rely on God to perfect our actions and must direct our lives toward him. What appears to us as good in the kingdom of the world may be imperfect or unworthy in the kingdom of God, to which believers aspire. Nothing can happen before it is meant to be. Therefore, we say in Sierra Leone that God's time is always ideal. Only God knows our purpose here on earth; hence we must render our best at all times and accept that *que será, será*: what will be, will be.

There is less reliance on the kingdom of God in Scandinavia. My friends there have greater belief in the human spirit than in spiritual miracles. In Sierra Leone, we believe in God and study Darwin, but the latter has assumed a higher place in Scandinavian society. I realized during my time in Norway that most people there believe in the power of their democratic welfare state more than in the idea of God. When one is hungry and homeless in Scandinavia, it is the state that one calls upon, not God. Once, during a discussion in my philosophy class at RCNUWC, we came across Nietzsche's declaration that "God is dead." I couldn't help but think to myself that if God is dead, he must have resurrected in Africa to a wild reception across the continent. The irony of God's resurrection in Africa is that it was in the name of God that the continent was enslaved, colonized, and exploited. But God, I believe, remains the only hope for many marginalized and underprivileged people of the kingdom of the world. I have often argued that Christianity and Islam thrive in Africa because our leaders are failing to uphold their end of our social contract. When citizens cannot afford to meet their basic needs and life is nothing but a bucket of misery, any God who promises paradise becomes a salvation, a *why* that offers the oppressed the strength to endure any *how*. Walk into any African megachurch and you will receive God on a platter of promised wealth, marriage, and power delivered through holy ointments paid for by hefty offerings. Yet there is no jar for a widow's farthing in many modern African churches.

"What happened? Did you get the visa?"

Erik was eager to know the outcome of my interview. The whole visa process seemed bizarre to him because Scandinavians do not have to obtain visas for short stays in the U.S., and visas to other countries are easily granted. Citizens of European countries that are members of the Schengen Agreement can travel freely within member states without a visa. The Schengen Agreement emerged from a 1985 Luxemburg Treaty and was subsequently incorporated into European Union laws by the Treaty of Amsterdam (1997), which abolished internal border controls and established a common visa policy for member states. Most young Europeans grew up in a region where they crossed national borders without even noticing. This is why Erik was uncomfortable about regulations that made it difficult for people from developing countries to travel through Western countries, especially when Westerners travel to many places around the world without much restriction.

"They are stupid rules, and someone should be able to do something," he said with a passionate dismissal upon hearing my news.

Erik had never given room to the thought that I might be denied a visa to the U.S. He had started to jokingly refer to me as an "American boy." I never tried to dampen his confidence that nothing could stop me, but I knew that my background might be an obstacle to obtaining a U.S. visa. Being a Sierra Leonean abroad after the civil war always generates two reactions: pity and the assumption of liability. Those with knowledge of the country's brutal civil war pity and sympathize with its citizens abroad, especially the refugees. But there are those who use that history to presume that Sierra Leoneans are liabilities who would deplete their country's resources. The fear that visitors will grab the resources of the host country is often the real underlying factor of most immigration debacles. A major argument of every anti-immigration debate occurring in modern states is that the immigrant is coming to take something away from the host country, be it jobs, education, housing, land, or whatever. I have even heard some nationalists claim that immigrant men come to take their wives. We are generally not afraid of others unless we feel we have something to lose, a privilege or possession threatened by the presence of others not like us. It is the same feeling that makes some children weep when they hear about the birth of a younger sibling.

I handed Erik the information paper I'd received from the embassy and awaited his reaction. After a brief reading, he let his arms fall in resignation as if to drop the paper from his hand.

"What the heck is 214b?" He was in need of an explanation.

Nothing but the liability, I thought before responding to Erik. "Well, basically the consular agent can use her discretion to presume me an immigrant instead of a temporary student," I said. Erik was not convinced. He was a strong believer in human rights, and Article Thirteen of the Universal Declaration of Human Rights, a document we had studied thoroughly at RCNUWC, grants all persons the right to freedom of movement and residence within the borders of each state and to leave and return to his country. To demonstrate to U.S. consular authorities one's "intention to leave," one must establish strong ties to one's country of origin that would convince a consular officer that one would leave the U.S. at the end of a temporary stay. Erik could not understand why such a discretionary rule should determine my eligibility for a visa, especially since I had a full scholarship to study in the U.S. I did not understand it either, but bureaucracies are not about bending rules, even when the cause is right. A couple of years in Norway seemed to have indicated a renunciation of strong ties to my country. The first commandment of bureaucracy is that those who do not fit into set rules must simply fall out. One would be lucky to find a bureaucrat who is willing to look beyond established rules. In Sierra Leone, we joke that bureaucrats are always "sorry for the inconvenience but never happy to help." I did everything I could have done to obtain a visa, but all I received was a meaningless stamp on the last page of my passport that read, "American Embassy, Oslo. Application Received on: May 27, 2004."

Erik wanted answers, and I had none. We exchanged intense looks, and I felt obliged to speak.

"Honestly, I don't know. But whatever the case, let's get out of here," I said. I wished to emphasize that there was nothing we could do at that moment to change the consul's decision. According to the paper describing the section of the U.S. Immigration Act under which I was denied a visa, I had a right to reapply if my situation changed—that is, if the embassy had told me something specific I could have done to comply. As far as I knew nothing was missing from my application. I had spent several days making sure that if I was denied a visa to the U.S., it wouldn't be as a result of anything I'd missed. My application was neat and complete. I looked it over and over until I knew all the sections and questions by heart.

Erik called his parents, who were driving to Oslo. They, too, were expecting news about the outcome of my visa interview. I stood by idly. Erik's parents had attended our graduation ceremony in Flekke, after which several of us classmates had taken the chartered bus to Oslo in order to be together one last time. I didn't understand Swedish very well, but I could hear that Erik's parents were equally displeased with the news and wanted an explanation. Erik read to them in his accented English: "Section 2. 1. 4. B. of U.S.A. Immigration Act paper."

Swedish and Norwegian sound similar to my ears, and I could never understand why students from both countries at RCNUWC teased each other about the phonetics of their languages. The same kind of teasing took place between Norwegian students who spoke Bokmål and those who spoke Nynorsk, New Norwegian. I had studied Nynorsk as a required class during my first year in Flekke. My random Norwegian vocabulary always amused friends I worked with at Operation Day's Work. They made me repeat words like *brunost, jordbaer, syltetoy, isbjørn*, and, my personal favorite, *tusen takk*—thank you. I said "Tusen takk" at the end of my presentations about the Sierra Leonean civil war to bring some laughter to the room. The story of the war was never a comfortable subject for young Norwegian students, who were far removed from the world's violence and deprivation. They would giggle as the phrase came out of my mouth smeared with an African accent. I always enjoy this aspect of being a foreigner—having the liberty to innocently butcher other people's languages.

Erik and I had a couple of hours to wait before his parents' arrival. Without saying anything, we both knew that we were not interested in sightseeing. We had been to Oslo before, and my unsuccessful visa application left both of us with a desire to brainstorm new ideas for my future. Erik had more questions about my visa, and I needed to think of my next strategy. The lady who interviewed me had asked if I couldn't apply in a neighboring country to Sierra Leone. The paper she gave me also stated that I could reapply if my situation changed. By combining these two factors and going to Guinea, my situation would have changed significantly. Besides, there was not much to lose by applying again, except of course another $100. I also intended to visit my mother and other family members in Guinea. With these ideas on my mind, I walked with Erik to a small park in the middle of Oslo to wait for his parents.

It was a sunny day. People went about their businesses with smiles on their faces. Several people were already sunbathing in the parks. Ever since I'd arrived in Norway, I'd learned to value a bright day. The only time we crave sunshine in Sierra Leone is during the rainy season, when people pray for the sun to emerge and dry their laundered clothes. But the sun, even in the summer, is valuable goods in Norway. Many Norwegians read the meteorological section of a newspaper before turning to the news. Friendly conversations almost always include a discussion of the weather predictions for the week. I did not worry much in the winters, because in Flekke it was permanently cold, dark, or rainy. The sun is expected to shine in the summer, but even then it may rain and remain cloudy for days. My Norwegian classmates told me that whatever the case may be, it is best to dress for the cold and reduce layers of clothing as needed. "There is no bad weather," they explained, "only bad clothing." That advice would later serve me well during my stay in upstate New York and Vermont. In locations that experience extreme winter weather, it is always better to remove layers than to be without.

"So what are you going to do now?" Erik asked as we made our way to a sunny area. I told him my plan of spending a few weeks in Sweden with him and then returning to Norway to live with my host family for a while before going home to Sierra Leone. I wanted to spend quality time with my Swedish and Norwegian surrogate families, just in case I never got to see them again. For a poor African, obtaining a visa to visit any European country is just as uncertain as getting one to visit the U.S. But this was not the information Erik was curious about. He wanted to know my new strategy to obtain a visa to the U.S., or whether I would consider attending college in Scandinavia. I had considered the University of Oslo, but I had done rather poorly in my *ab initio* Norwegian class, which overruled any practical desire to pursue a bachelor's degree in Norway. My Norwegian visa was set to expire before the end of the year. I could not see any viable route to a Scandinavian option.

Erik was still visibly affected by my failed visa application. He was, in his own words, pissed. After a while, I told my friend in a jovial manner to stop worrying and think about how much fun we were going to have together in Åhus, his hometown. Erik was familiar with my levelheaded approach to crisis, and he understood my need for time to figure things out. He smiled and gave me a hug.

Erik is proud of having been born in Åhus, which is also home to the Absolut vodka distillery. He says the town has something for everyone. He is fascinated that the Absolut plant resembles the biggest church in Åhus. He even has a painting in his kitchen of the two structures. "This is the God church, and this is the vodka church," he says. He loves to point out their architectural similarities, as if to coax me toward a deeper philosophy. They are two important buildings that certainly render their services to Åhus: one purifies its soul, and the other enlivens its body. Most inhabitants of the world appreciate the existence of the vodka church. They may never visit Åhus, but they partake of the "communion" spirit from its vodka church in abundance.

I like to tell people all over the world that I have been in the vodka church. Although I did not observe any direct link between it and the God church, it is quite evident that the vodka church is prospering as membership in the God church dwindles. A friend told me that in Scandinavia expected attendance at the God church is a matter of trinity: birth, marriage, and death. In Sierra Leone, God church—mosque or shrine—is a matter of daily life. Even those who frequent the local vodka churches pay their dues to God by attending one of his houses, albeit sometimes drunk.

There are always stories of heads of various God churches in Sierra Leone conducting services just after a visit to a vodka church. My favorite involved my cousin Pascal and his pastor, who was a Nigerian born-again preacher. The pastor commissioned Pascal to drum during the praise-and-worship segment of his Sunday services for a small fee subtracted from the collection. Pascal was not a devout Christian, but he needed the money. The pastor did not always pay Pascal's commission on time, and he often disappeared at the end of the service. One Sunday, Pascal ran into the pastor at a pub on Lumley Beach, on the west coast of Freetown.

"Pastor, na you dis?"—is that you?—he asked in Krio.

"My friend, don't call me 'pastor' in this place!" the pastor whispered to him.

Many people took to the vodka churches in Sierra Leone after the civil war because they felt that God had abandoned them during the war. It is the capitulating creed on Calvary: "Eli, Eli, lama sabachthani?" My God, my God, why have you forsaken me? Some of those who believed in God before the war and lost everything in the war could no longer find consolation in the God churches. Their consolation lay instead in the vodka church, where salvation is bought in liters and everyone is his own vicar. They drink and condemn everything from the government to imperialism. Sometimes we blame it on the amount of liquor in their heads, but it is indeed what is in the head when there is no wine in the head that comes out when there *is* wine in the head. The problem in Sierra Leone is that, unlike in Scandinavia, a visit to the vodka church often requires a man to choose between feeding his family and drinking his life away, or what we referred to as "drowning in the bottle." Brawls sometimes break out as women charge into local *omorlay* corners, makeshift pubs, to drag their husbands home. Several marriages have been shattered by men's devotion to the vodka church.

The question of God, like everything in Sierra Leone, is full of contradictions and double standards. There is confusion especially among Christians on the question of what a Christian should not do and what's expected from the kingdom of the world versus the kingdom of God. We joke that if God is against the vodka church, why did Jesus perform his first miracle by turning water into wine, not soup. One would think that a man at a party who is against drunkenness would not serve the best wine. But my own dilemma as a Sierra Leonean today lies in the fact that many people sin against God out of desperation and hopelessness. Could the generals who control everything in the kingdom of the world undergo the same eschatological judgment as their foot soldiers, those who have to kill, steal, or lie to preserve their own lives? I ask this question on behalf of child soldiers who are conscripted to fight in meaningless wars, pickpockets whose very right to life depends on whatever they snatch from others, and corrupt civil servants whose sole purpose for doing what they do is to live for another day. These are all morally wrong acts by human standards, but does God apply the same measure of judgment as man? Do we vindicate God by accepting that we are mere forlorn creatures living the anguish of our individual choices? Otherwise, are we doomed in a Sartrean sense that we can always choose, with the awareness that by not choosing we make a choice? This is a dilemma that confronts anyone caught in the web of good and evil, whether he believes in God or not.

Ulla and Magnus, Erik's parents, picked us up at the park in Oslo. Ever since I celebrated Christmas with Erik's family in 2002, my freshman year at RCNUWC, I am always glad to see Ulla and Magnus. It was my first time celebrating Christmas outside Africa, and it was a wonderful experience. I was happy to do without the long Christmas-morning sermons and listen instead to the wonderful stories of Erik's family. Erik's relatives are world travelers, and that meant hearing interesting tales of their experiences across the globe. Ulla had done preliminary research on the kinds of food people eat in Sierra Leone. Eggplant is one of the vegetables on the list she obtained. Little did Ulla know that eggplant is the one vegetable I disliked. But how on earth was I going to tell my host that I detested eggplant after she went to all that trouble to find it in Åhus? I never told her, and I got used to eating eggplant and learned to like it. I believe that when others go all out for me, I should compromise, especially where there is no danger to my health or life. I disliked eggplant as a matter of taste only, not health, so there was no difficulty adjusting the buds in gratitude to my hosts.

Magnus enjoyed teasing me about my journey from Sierra Leone, a warm country, to Norway. He made sure that there was enough wood for the fireplace every time I visited. He gave me the nickname "Fireman," meaning I was responsible for keeping the fire burning in the fireplace. This was the only job required of me in Åhus; everything else was taken care of by Magnus and Ulla. Erik and I could sleep as long as we needed—well, at least until Ulla decided enough was enough. I was usually awake before she came in, but Erik always needed Ulla, then Magnus, and then me to harass him before he would get up. It was my duty to wake Erik when we were in Flekke; otherwise he might never have gotten out of bed. I learned my first Swedish phrase in return for waking Erik up: *fa faen*—fuck! Erik was not a morning person, and that was clearly expressed whenever he had to get up early. After weeks of hearing him utter "Fa faen!" before struggling out of bed, I asked what it meant.

"Just don't let my mom ever hear you use it," Erik said to me.

"Great translation!" I joked, having realized what the phrase means.

We related to Erik's parents in detail the ordeals of my morning in the embassy. Magnus expressed his disappointment, and Ulla asked her usual question whenever I am caught in a dilemma: "Oh, Joseph, what are we going to do now?"

"We will go to Åhus," I joked. Everyone laughed. I wanted the laughter to divert our minds from the unfavorable outcome of my visa interview. We drove to a McDonald's to get some burgers before boarding a ship to Sweden. Erik and I complained about eating at McDonald's, but Ulla and Magnus were not convinced by what they called our "idealist United World College argument." We talked a lot about Morgan Spurlock's documentary film *Super Size Me*—a personal experiment on the effects of fast food on the body and mind. Magnus reminded us that there are strict food regulations in Scandinavia, and the ills depicted in *Super Size Me* are American problems. There is no unhealthful supersization in Scandinavia!

Ulla and Magnus had arranged for us to join a cruise ferry that was on its way to Denmark via Sweden. I was fascinated with this village on the sea; I had never been on a cruise ferry. There were hundreds of cars and motorbikes parked belowdecks. Above, hundreds of people milled about in the multiple shopping centers, bars, and restaurants. It didn't feel like we were even at sea. Every time I encounter a complex human invention like a ship or an airplane, I can't help but think of the rough edges of the world that we have failed to straighten. I wonder whether it is a lack of ability or mere negligence that makes us ignore the sight of poverty, wars, and diseases. What I know is that these are not the greatest challenges to human inventive power. We debated such questions at RCNUWC during two biannual conferences called Global Concerns. A mini version of Global Concerns took place in a weekly forum called World Today. But school was over, so I had to relax and enjoy the cruise.

We enjoyed a sumptuous family dinner before going to bed. Erik and I shared a room with two bunk beds. We had still not gotten over the disappointment from the morning. I hoped it would not overshadow our stay in Åhus. There is no use in mourning forever the things we cannot change. We talked very little before falling asleep.

We arrived in Sweden very early the next morning. We were delayed on board by dozens of motorbikes that were parked in front of the cars, but they eventually rushed out like an army of ants. We drove a short distance to reach Åhus.

Åhus is a town in Kristianstad municipality, Skåne County, southern Sweden. It has approximately ten thousand regular inhabitants but sees a significant population increase in the summer, when tourists frequent the area to enjoy the waterfront and beaches. One of the oldest buildings in Åhus is Sankta Maria Kyrka, St. Mary's Church—in other words, the God church. The town is also known among Swedes and tourists for its eel parties, *ålagille*, when people assemble to eat eel and drink schnapps. Åhus is known as the origin of the so-called three Swedish sins: snuff, schnapps, and eel. In the 1800s, tobacco and eel production were high, bestowing the town with a "Cigar King" and an "Eel King." The Eel King supplied the Swedish royal family with eel, while the Cigar King, Per Svensson, oversaw the production of "Åhus Havanas." But nothing in Åhus' hall of fame surpasses the global reach of Absolut vodka, which is entirely produced in the small town using what the company calls the One Source Concept: one local distillery, locally grown wheat, and water from a local source. *Ça veut dire*, Absolut vodka is absolutely produced in Åhus.

In the spirit of camaraderie that I have consistently experienced in Åhus, friends of Erik came from every corner to say hello and join in brainstorming about my future. Some of them I had met during my previous visit to Åhus, but others I was meeting for the first time. There was Peter, at whose house we spent some of our afternoons watching soccer or talking about the leagues. There were also Pop, who brought me new clothes and candy every time I visited Åhus, and his wife, Agnet. Thanks to Pop, I did not purchase any clothing for myself until I was a junior in college. Many other friends visited, too. I always enjoy returning to Åhus, that beautiful Swedish town I feel lucky to call my second home.

CHAPTER 5

Kindness is like a seed sown; no
matter how small, it has the potential
to grow into something big.

I was in Åhus to celebrate graduating from high school, an important occasion for Scandinavian students that involves a period of partying. The rituals include, as they say in Swedish, *röka, kröka, pöka* (smoke, drink, and sex). Every graduate is expected to organize a party and invite the other graduates. Pulling off this feat can be complicated, as everyone tries to avoid scheduling conflicts with the others in their class, especially the popular ones. Some students postpone their parties until graduation fever is over and more classmates are available to attend. The only difficulty with postponing a party is that the organizational requirements grow: one needs to provide more drinks, a bigger space, and a great band, because more classmates are usually available to attend events scheduled for a few weeks after graduation.

The RCNUWC academic calendar is shorter than the Swedish one, so Erik and I graduated earlier than most students in Sweden. Some of Erik's friends were still taking classes or exams when we arrived in Åhus. Ulla had decided to throw a graduation party for us, and we were quite excited about the event. Planning it was loads of work, but Ulla knew to start early enough to distribute the burden over an extended period. All Erik had to do was tell her whom and what he wanted at the party, and I just had to be present. Ulla made sure I felt at home by regularly asking whether there was anything I needed. I love candy, so that was a guarantee each time she went to the supermarket. "Joseph, is there anything else you want for the party—apart from candy, of course?"

My friend Pop had sent Erik and me a large box of candy when we were still in Flekke. Erik ate very little of the candy out of concern for his teeth, but, like a child, I had no such worry. Erik was fascinated by the fact that I had never visited a dentist, and candy is my favorite snack, yet my teeth are strong. I joked that my toothbrush is my dentist and I use my money for candy. I learned that in many Western countries, regular visits to the dentist are a health expectation. Most Sierra Leoneans never visit a dentist or any other health professional unless they are stricken by a debilitating illness. It is difficult to persuade poor people to pay for preventative measures against ailments they do not yet suffer. In Sierra Leone, oftentimes, by the time sickness strikes, it is too late to pursue an affordable remedy.

I was not the only candy lover in Åhus. Magnus ate lots of candy too, but I noticed that he liked chocolates, and I liked the ones with a high sugar concentration. Swedish fish and gummy bears are a delight. I would later acquire a taste for *läkerol*, but I hadn't yet. Every now and then, Magnus looked through my candy bowl and picked out his favorites, including my abandoned *läkerols*.

Ulla needed to buy food for the house and the party. Frosted Flakes, my favorite breakfast cereal, was on the list. No one else ate it, so it had to be purchased every time I was in Åhus. Erik and I were invited to accompany Ulla shopping. Erik drove her car, and he playfully complained about the lack of legroom in the driver's seat. Ulla is a small woman, but her husband and four sons are rather tall. She responded to Erik's complaint with a counterclaim that the last time Erik drove her car, he had pushed the seat way back and taken her CDs. While we drove, Ulla introduced us to the music of Eva Cassidy, an American vocalist and guitarist who had recently obtained posthumous fame in Europe. Erik later uploaded her album *Songbird* to my MP3 player, and I remember listening to the track "Fields of Gold" on repeat for months. We drove around

Åhus on our way to the supermarket, listening to Cassidy and some of Erik's favorite Swedish folk songs, jokingly accusing and counteraccusing each other.

As Ulla shopped, Erik and I pushed the cart behind her. Ulla turned to me on every other aisle to ask if I saw anything I wanted. She was unaware of how the supermarket overwhelmed me. Even after two years in Scandinavia, I was still adjusting from my days of unmet needs in Sierra Leone to the present luxury of abundance. I never asked for anything except cereal and white bread. Those two items were my only food preferences that Ulla didn't regularly keep on hand. I would later learn that my choices of candy, sugary cereals, and white bread were not considered a healthy diet, but that did not bother me. My unhealthy food choices were counterbalanced by Ulla's sumptuous meals. Life in Sweden was never a struggle for daily bread; it was about making choices in the presence of plentiful food. Unlike my former life in Sierra Leone, I never woke up in Scandinavia worrying whether I would have a meal or not.

Shopping in the supermarket of Åhus was an interesting social experience. Curious shoppers watched me from the corners of their eyes. They gave me the sort of look that seemed to amusingly wonder whether I had taken a wrong turn and landed in their homogeneous town. *How did he get here? What is he doing here? Who is he with?* their eyes queried as they walked by, trying hard not to be conspicuous. I was never offended by their stares, because the chances of seeing a black person in Åhus are very slight, and if a Caucasian suddenly showed up in Sierra Leone, I would do the same. I must admit, the gazes of the Swedish shoppers were far better than having a group of children singing behind a Caucasian visitor on every corner of a town in Sierra Leone. Growing up there, the only Caucasians I ever saw were missionaries or Peace Corps volunteers. My parents hosted Caucasian Peace Corps volunteers when my father was a lecturer at Bunumbu Teachers College. When Caucasians visit their villages, Sierra Leonean children follow behind them and scream,

"White person!" in the local language. A Caucasian friend once returned from East Africa with nostalgia for her acquired celebrity title: *muzungu*. Wherever she visited, children gathered to chant, *"Muzungu, muzungu, muzungu."* My parents never allowed us to participate in the game of yelling while following Caucasians, but even if I'd been allowed, I would not have done it. I preferred looking at Caucasians from a distance, observing their gestures, the way they spoke English, the simplicity of their clothing, and the color of their eyes. I was fascinated by Caucasians but too shy to ever get close to them.

My friends and I had our own childhood theories of who Caucasians really were. They must have died and been reincarnated with white bodies. Their language was not English; it sounded like the whispers of the local masquerade devils. They were spirits from the underworld. Another theory was that Caucasians, especially Caucasian women, were *mami water*, goddesses of the sea. Most Sierra Leonean children grow up believing in this spirit entity. She is white. There are several stories about her powers, but a prominent one is that she loves handsome men. Whenever a man drowns, we believe that he has been chosen by *mami water*, the beautiful white goddess of the sea. I once told this story to a Caucasian friend who visited me in Sierra Leone, and she asked whether *mami water* would be interested in her. I responded that she probably wasn't gay.

Our parents warned us strictly against swimming in any river. It is a warning I never adhered to. I was often in trouble because I swam every time we went to the river to do laundry. With our eyes reddened from long hours of swimming, it was easy for our parents to detect what we had been up to.

I don't accept the idea that children should dance behind their Caucasian visitors as though they were new masquerade masks at the town square, but that seems to be their way of expressing a sincere sense of wonder. I believe the children scream due to their fascination with "otherness." It is generally as adults that we develop prejudices based on the color of people's skin and other such qualities. I have always rejected skin color or race as a determinant of character. I see people as people, in spite of our multiple colors. This is perhaps the reason why living in a predominantly Caucasian community has never bothered me. The only measure of a human being should be what I often describe as the King Standard, based on Dr. King's dream for his children to live in a nation where they are judged not by the color of their skin but by the content of their character.

Sometimes I made eye contact with the people in the supermarket in Åhus and smiled, especially at the children. Some of the smaller children got scared and moved closer to their parents while still trying to establish familiarity; others smiled so wide that I often got pulled into a game of trading smiles between the aisles. We sometimes played these games without the knowledge of the busy parents, rushing to grab their groceries. Some of the children would turn around and wave good-bye as they followed their parents out of the supermarket. In their tender years, they were not threatened by my presence; they were healthily curious. Their young minds had not been sullied by the pollutants of racial prejudice that limit diverse communities across the world.

While interacting with friends of Erik and his parents, I got used to answering questions about home, food, my disdain or love for Scandinavian weather, and the safety of my family in Sierra Leone. Those who were informed about my visit had already done some research on Sierra Leone. I was grateful for the fact that people I was meeting for the first time already knew something about my country. They tried to clarify some of their questions on the civil war and how I'd made it out alive. I could only imagine their shock as they googled Sierra Leone for the first time. In the years immediately following the end of the conflict, only gruesome images of amputees and dreadful-looking child soldiers appeared in search engines. Communication was usually not a problem, since almost everyone in Sweden speaks English, even if with some difficulty. I was always entirely engaged with the conversation because I was, rightly so, expected to fill in an occasional missing English word or correct an improperly used phrase. Erik also helped to translate from Swedish, but sometimes I understood what was being said. I had learned some Swedish words from Erik and other Swedes at RCNUWC.

I used Erik's laptop computer to do my academic work at RCNUWC. The computer was programmed in Swedish, and nobody knew how to change it to English, so I had to learn some Swedish vocabulary to operate it. Sometimes I asked Erik what a word or phrase meant, but often he did not know the English equivalent. He usually tried to explain through hand gestures and sound effects that were worse than my Swedish. I lost a few unsaved papers, but by the end of our time in Flekke I had memorized just enough Microsoft prompts in Swedish to use the computer without Erik's help.

Erik, like most RCNUWC students, except those who were from English-speaking countries, spoke little English during his first year at the school. However, English-language assistance was available to all the students. Students also study their own languages as self-taught subjects with the assistance of a native-speaking teacher either in Flekke or through a distance-learning scheme. I helped Erik edit his English essays. Isabel, Erik's girlfriend, who was also from Sweden but spoke fluent English, was my assistant on days when I was too busy to tutor. I enjoyed helping Erik with his English essays. I liked his expressive reactions whenever we came up with the right word, given that my own English vocabulary had had to undergo some transformation in Flekke. When I went to Norway, my grammar was certainly better than my lexicon.

"Damn, you are smart, man!" Erik exclaimed whenever I explained why one of his words could not be used in a particular sentence.

We left the supermarket with all kinds of food. Ulla had already completed the other arrangements for the party: music, drinks, and an outdoor tent. It was summertime, and the weather was usually nice, but counting on sunshine is a gamble in Scandinavia. One is better off preparing for rain. Magnus was responsible for making sure that everything in the house was working properly. Ulla was very excited to host the party, and Erik was looking forward to a good time with family and friends. Invitations were sent out, and guests called to RSVP. We were pretty sure that everything would go well. The only other issue we had to take care of was to buy me a blazer.

A few days before the big event, nearly everything was in place, except for the details Ulla wanted to improve: moving an object from one part of the house to another, or getting some forgotten spices that might add a little more flavor to certain dishes. Erik and I rushed to the supermarket to buy whatever Ulla needed. Erik, like me, was bad at food shopping, even when his mother wrote the desired ingredients on paper. I could not help because I don't even know the names of most spices in English, let alone Swedish, but we always managed to find the necessary one. The principle "when in doubt, ask the closest shopper" always works. I am also terrible at finding my way around new places. I am the sort who takes the wrong turn even with a GPS in hand. Over the years, I have figured out that asking a street vendor always saves me from getting lost.

I was looking forward to a night of food, drinks, and new friends. It felt good to shift from working hard in Flekke to the pleasure of life without homework, school meetings, projects, and Extended Essays. The International Baccalaureate–required Extended Essay is an independent research paper of four thousand words—the bane of our RCNUWC senior year. With the IB mock exams and final exams behind us, I was excited to celebrate, but a few days before the party I woke up to the sad news that Magnus' father had passed away in Kinna, a town a little north of Åhus. There would be no party. Ulla and Magnus attended the funeral, and Erik and I stayed home. At least we didn't have to go grocery shopping or cook. There was enough food and drink in the house to tide us over while his parents were away, but we were consumed by sorrow. We said very little

71

to each other about the party. We simply ate, drank, and watched movies. Sometimes we invited Peter and other friends over for video games and food. Other times we went to nearby Kristianstad to see a movie. Or we played soccer when I was not watching Erik play tennis, his favorite sport. *Why did Magnus' father have to die now?* I thought to myself to pass the silent moments. But normal people do not live life thinking of when they will die, and unless it's by suicide or a terminal illness, we hardly know when or how we will leave this earth.

I had met Erik's grandfather once, when he visited Ulla and Magnus for a few days. He spoke softly and briefly. I could tell that he wanted to have a longer conversation with me, but age was weighing on him. He was over ninety, and even his hearing aid was not doing its job very well anymore. His death was a puzzle to me, not because of the life lost, but because of the way it was handled—quietly. When a Mende person or a Kissi person (a person from my mother's ethnicity) dies, it is a moment of great sorrow regardless of their age. People wail while they walk miles and miles to reach the funeral home. In places where there are no funeral homes, people sleep on a mat beside their dead. Relatives mourn for weeks and in some instances months. People grieve the dead as if it were their first realization of death. I am often fascinated by those who cry through songs, reciting eulogies in melody and tears. A few even attempt to jump into the grave of their dead relative. Someone always restrains them, but I find myself wondering if they really would follow through and leap. When an important person dies, Kissi people often invite professional mourners to sing ballads and entertain other mourners.

But like every aspect of Sierra Leonean traditional life, there is discipline, even at a funeral. Ample time is allowed to mourn the dead, but dramatizing sorrow or overacting pain is scorned. Some mourners get slapped by elder women for repeatedly trying to jump into the grave and disrupting the funeral rites. Those who are too hardheaded for scolding get their legs and hands tied and are placed into a room guarded by an elder who escorts them to the bathroom or brings them food. Men are not expected to cry, although exceptions are made based on the circumstance of the death. A man whose wife dies during childbirth is permitted to cry, perhaps because he is seen as cursed by God or witchcraft. Unusual deaths, which include occurrences such as death by an unknown disease, death in pregnancy, a fall from a palm tree while tapping palm wine, death during sex, or sudden death without illness, are often attributed to enemy attack through witchcraft or a punishment from the gods. It is mostly at such funerals that one sees men crying, albeit in a manly manner—tears only.

Ulla and Magnus returned to Åhus a few days later to take us to Kinna for a family gathering. Everything concerning the funeral was over. We were there to be together. The conversation was mostly in Swedish, so I was left out. I knew the discussion was not relevant to me; otherwise Erik would have translated for me. We left Kinna the same day and returned to Åhus. It was a long ride, but whenever we were together, time went quickly. We talked about everything, including what Erik and I had been up to without Ulla and Magnus. I don't think they were impressed by our routine: playing the FIFA video game, soccer, tennis, and eating. We arrived in Åhus late, and everyone was tired enough to go directly to bed. But as usual, Ulla made sure that we didn't retire hungry—no one is allowed to do that whenever Ulla is around. Erik used to warn me, "Joseph, when my mama says eat, you *have* to eat." I usually complied.

I spent the rest of my time in Åhus attending graduation parties with Erik. Once, we took a wrong turn on our drive to another Swedish RCNUWC classmate's party and drove around beautiful farmlands for hours. The cows were so healthy and handsome that they could have been on the label of *La vache qui rit* cheese. We took a trip to

Copenhagen to visit Vijay and Nikolai, whom I had studied philosophy with. Vijay is an American, but he decided to move to Copenhagen after graduation. Nikolai is Danish. We spent the day talking about our time in Flekke and learning the unofficial history of Denmark from Nikolai. It was a very beautiful summer day, and the streets of the city were crowded with people. The phrase "make hay while the sun shines" holds a certain practical meaning in Scandinavia.

I became thirsty after a long walk. I didn't have any Danish kroner, so I asked Nikolai to buy me a bottle of water. Nikolai told me in a very funny tone of voice that it was much more cost-effective for him to buy me a beer than a bottle of water, because the latter was more expensive in Copenhagen. I was not yet the beer lover I have since become, so Nikolai was hinting at the notion that I was visiting a country with *probably the best beer in the world* and I needed to adjust.

Nikolai told us that a tour of Copenhagen is incomplete without a visit to Christiania. An aspect of Christiania I loved even before visiting it is that residents call it Freetown. Although it does not resemble the capital city of Sierra Leone, the Freetown of Copenhagen upholds the true meaning of its name. Christiania or Freetown is an autonomous area of about eighty-five acres in the heart of Copenhagen that hosts nearly a thousand inhabitants. The settlers consider themselves residents of a free world outside Denmark and the European Union. Christianites, as residents are called, have no formal government and obey no official constitution beyond a few communal rules. Christiania is a home for nonconformists—a refuge for those who need a community that is an alternative to a highly regulated, individualistic society.

Settlement of Christiania started in the 1970s, when a few Copenhagen residents converted an old military facility into a playground for their children. The area was gradually occupied by squatters, hippies, and others who wanted to create an unconventional living space. The settlement exists to "create and sustain a self-governing community, in which everyone is free to develop and express themselves as responsible members of the community." After several failed attempts by the Danish government to evict the settlers, Christiania was approved as a social-experiment commune. It has become a symbol of diversity, tolerance, and environmentally conscious living in spite of periodic disagreements with various Danish governments throughout its existence. There have been recent attempts to close the settlement, but Christianites have fought hard for their communal survival.

Residents were forced to establish simple expectations that closely resemble the Golden Rule rather than traditional laws. They have a modern Green Plan that encourages residents to maintain low ecological footprints. No hard drugs, stolen goods, bikers' colors, sale of fireworks, use of thunderflashes, bulletproof clothing, weapons, or violence is allowed in the settlement. No private cars are allowed, either. The only means of transportation is the Christiania bike, a unique cargo-capable tricycle produced in the settlement. These constitute the nine rules of the Christiania Common Law, established to counteract some serious crimes that almost wrecked the settlement in its early days. Visitors are encouraged to recycle anything that is recyclable, and to use public toilets instead of nature.

We visited Christiania in the evening, when most outsiders went there to enjoy what the official bulletin refers to as a "magic mixture of anarchy and love." A guide told us that a major social infraction in Christiania would be letting one's tree grow so high as to block the neighbors' sunlight. The rule does not set out to regulate the height of trees; it aims to protect everyone's right to sunshine. Erik, Vijay, Nikolai, and I sat quietly in a small park close to the main entrance. I lifted my head toward the gate, and my eyes caught a warning: "You are now entering the EU." It is a reminder that residents' freedom is subject to restrictions beyond the gate. The world on the other side functions on a social contract that sacrifices individual freedom for structure. Fear of a Hobbesian state of nature in which life is "solitary, poor, nasty, brutish, and short" provides uncontestable reasons to surrender individual freedoms to collective governments, even when such governments become tyrannical and unrepresentative of the people.

The dichotomy of human existence in Copenhagen made me wonder whether our quest for a perfect society everywhere has in fact warranted too many unnecessary restrictions on freedom and creativity. Democracy has become a convenient political system in which the regulars are reelected and the voice of the people no longer echoes in the temples of government or law. Why should residents of Copenhagen escape to Christiania to experience freedom? Is it possible to make Christiania a social experiment for other places in the world? Can we trust ourselves with absolute freedom? As I walked through the gate of Christiania back into Copenhagen and the EU, I became conscious of the fact that I was entering a different territory where, unlike the Freetown of Christiania, I was subject to discrimination, prejudice, and perhaps even "random" interrogation by the security apparatus of an organized state.

Erik and I returned to Åhus at the end of our day in Denmark. Visiting Vijay and Nikolai had lifted my spirit. I used to enjoy debating God, morality, and ethics with them. Nikolai was also a fine guitarist and a founding member of SAFUGE. Apart from the extended philosophical conversations I had with Vijay, he also offered to adopt me as his brother if I was otherwise unable to obtain a U.S. visa. "It is ironic that I am running away from my country to live freely elsewhere, and they are denying you entrance, my friend," he said to me.

Vijay was one of the first people to ever call me a "good man." I grew up in societies where only chiefs, ministers, and presidents are told that they are good. The goodness of an ordinary person is only recited at his funeral. Those genuine appreciations and appraisals by Vijay and others I have met on my journey always inspire me to do better, even though I blush each time I receive such a compliment. I subscribe to the view that we should give flowers while the recipient can still water them, not to encourage vainglory, but in sincere acknowledgment of those who make our world better. Most people who do good unto others do so for the inherent value of the service to the recipient. It is up to us to remind our inspired protagonists that their services make the world a better place. I usually tell my American friends who lament the small size of their donations to my work in Sierra Leone to leave it to those in need to determine the real value of their generosity. Kindness is like a seed sown; no matter how small, it has the potential to grow into something big.

After a few weeks in Sweden, I was ready to return to Norway to spend time with my host family. As usual, Pop brought a bag of clothes and assorted candies for me. Ulla organized a farewell dinner. We ate together and talked about my plans for the future. I was hopeful that I would be able to obtain a U.S. visa in West Africa. Things ahead were promising, even if the question of entering the U.S. remained unresolved. I still could not understand why I had been unable to obtain a visa in Oslo, so I did not know what to change before I made another attempt in Africa, but attempt I would.

We agreed that I would pursue my plan to return to Sierra Leone and reapply, in either Guinea, Gambia, or Senegal, but Erik wanted to know why I was so optimistic about obtaining the visa in West Africa when I hadn't been able to get it in Oslo. I didn't really know the answer, but I had to try. Losing one battle in the struggle for my future does not end the war. I don't believe in stopping an endeavor before all possible avenues have been explored. I am a survivor, and life has taught me to try and try again. Maybe at some point someone would tell me what I needed to change or do to obtain a U.S. visa, but until then I had to keep trying—unless of course I no longer had another $100 to pay for my attempt.

CHAPTER 6

When the journey gets tough, always remember why you're on the road in the first place.

Before I left Sweden, Erik and I decided that I could return for higher education if the U.S. option failed, or his parents could help me in other ways. Magnus gave me some money he had converted to pounds sterling (I had told him that pounds are worth more than dollars in Sierra Leone). Ulla made sure I had sandwiches for the flight from Sweden to Norway. We drove to the airport without saying much, this time out of the sadness of separation. We hugged each other outside the Kristianstad Airport, and then Magnus walked me through security. The process was easy, perhaps because the airport is rather small and the number of passengers going through was low. It was the first time on my journey that I walked through airport security in less than five minutes. It has never happened again. I have now become a permanent member of the "randomly selected passenger" club, which means that I am often an African passport–carrying recipient of shoulder-to-toe pat downs or X-ray exhibitions for tense security personnel. Once, in a U.S. airport, to the amusement of other travelers, I let my pants drop right in front of an officer ready to frisk me. I was not traveling commando that day.

My flight to Stockholm took a little over an hour. I joined a connecting flight to Oslo, where I caught a bus to Førde, Norway—half an hour away from Sande, home of Desiree and Inge, my Norwegian host mother and father. Even though RCNUWC is a boarding school, some students are assigned host families whom they can visit on designated weekends. I had traveled the road between Oslo and Førde many times before, but I am always awed by the beauty of Norway's roads that wind through mountain ranges, dimly lit tunnels, and stave churches. I have visited a few places around the world, but I have never seen any terrain as mind-blowing as the Norwegian landscape and its astonishing architecture. Every corner or crevice of Norway left me with a heavenly awe.

I arrived in Førde the following morning and called Inge to pick me up from the bus station. He showed up about an hour later, and we drove home together. Anna Kamilla and Elias, my host sister and brother, were glad to see me. Desiree had given birth to twins in May, so I now also had two baby brothers, Johannes and Jacob.

I was happy to be back in Sande, a small town with a grocery store, a church, and a school. I had visited for weekends many times before and had come to know many friends of Desiree and Inge. This time I was there for the rest of the summer. I was particularly excited about spending time with the twins. I find joy in being with babies and children, and I was looking forward to babysitting my host brothers and sister. Even though I didn't speak Norwegian and Anna Kamilla and Elias didn't speak English, we had little difficulty communicating with each other, or so I thought until the day that I unintentionally made Anna Kamilla cry.

I was used to responding to questions from the kids with "*ja*" or "*nei.*" Many times I answered even when I didn't completely comprehend the question, but went by chance and intuition. One day Anna Kamilla came over to me and asked in her usual sweet and gentle manner, "Joseph, skal du har is?" Joseph, would you like ice cream?

"Nei, Anna Kamilla." Thinking it was one of the questions children ask without needing an answer, I responded without understanding what she had said. Anna Kamilla went back to Desiree with tears in her eyes because I had refused an offer of ice cream.

When Desiree explained that I was responsible for my little sister's tears, and what had gone missing in the translation, I was heartbroken. I convinced Anna Kamilla, or Desiree helped me explain, that what I'd really meant to say was yes. Anna Kamilla was satisfied, and we both enjoyed the ice cream on that hot summer day. Thereafter, I tried never to answer *ja* or *nei* without understanding at least a part of the question. Besides this incident, we understood each other most of the time, even if we ended up entertaining the adults with the silliness of our conversations. Sometimes Desiree or Inge translated for us. The kids were much more confident in attempting to speak English than I Norwegian, even after my two years in Norway. I had dropped my Norwegian class after the mandatory semester, contrary to the advice of my teacher, who believed I could do better, and enrolled in a Spanish class.

My return to Norway was purely for vacation and to spend time with my host family, but I tried to engage myself as much as possible, especially with the children. I babysat whenever Desiree and Inge were busy or visiting neighbors. Anna Kamilla and Elias were more comfortable talking and interacting with me when their parents weren't around. Sometimes they were helpful with the twins, who were difficult to pacify when they were hungry. They attempted to suckle on any part of my face they could reach. One would attempt to reach for my nose while I was trying to get the other off my ear. Then they would both start to scream at the top of their small lungs. At this point, I felt rather defeated by two tiny human beings. A hungry baby is an angry baby who won't stop crying no matter what one does short of offering food. Elias or Anna Kamilla would call Desiree for me, and she wasted no time in responding. Inge was also sympathetic to my plight. I think they may have attempted to munch his face, too.

Desiree decided to give me a job that Inge had been postponing: chopping wood for the winter. I was happy to have a chore when Desiree and Inge were busy and the twins were asleep. I had lifted weights when I was a student in Flekke, but I had not done any lifting since graduation, and I felt weak. The manual labor of chopping wood with an axe gave me a surge of adrenaline that kept me going until Desiree appeared to make me take a break: "Joseph, we are having some sandwiches now."

After lunch I organized the wood nicely in the shed. Chopping wood also offered a time for reflection. I thought of the things I had done and the things I needed to do, where I had been and where I was going. I reflected on the gift of love I was receiving so far from home, and on the people I had met in Scandinavia who treated me no differently than my family at home. I thought about the smiles I exchanged with Anna Kamilla, who sometimes came to inform me that food was ready, and Elias, who always found it incredible that I had chopped all the wood around me. Elias dreamed of having my kind of biceps when he grew older. When I first met Elias and Anna Kamilla, they'd been five and four. Desiree had asked Anna Kamilla whether it was all right that I would be staying in her room for a weekend.

"Well, where else would he sleep?"

Whereas some children might have objected to a stranger taking over their room, Anna Kamilla was surprised that her mother had even asked. I later showed Anna Kamilla a video of an African woman carrying her child on her back. I didn't think she would make much of the video, until she started requesting a piggyback ride from her African brother. She wanted a piggyback ride again, and again, and again, as children often do when they love something. Anna Kamilla had me with her cuteness, and she got her rides.

Desiree thought I should make some money before returning to West Africa. I did not object, because I needed the funds. I accepted a job doing some touch-up painting on the exterior of the home of our neighbors Vidar and Ingunn. I let them pay me whatever amount they deemed appropriate, because I would have done it free of charge. We had become friends during my visits to Sande, and I had been raised not to accept money from neighbors for helping with house chores or farming. Vidar compensated me with a few hundred kroner that he gave to Desiree, knowing that I might have turned the money down if he'd given it straight to me.

I also helped Desiree's brother refurbish a house he had recently purchased in Sande. One day, we took a break from laying hardwood floors, and I drank a cold peach drink. A few minutes later I felt a familiar nausea. I knew what would follow, so I told Desiree's brother to take me home. By the time we got to Desiree's house, a short distance away, my body temperature had gone through the roof. I was shivering and my breath was hot, while at the same time sweating under the many blankets Desiree had thrown on me. I hadn't had malaria for many years, but there could not have been any other cause for this fever.

Desiree observed the severity of my symptoms. When Inge walked into the room, she asked him what they should do.

"It's malaria. Take me to the hospital," I said through trembling lips.

"Ah, malaria!" Desiree reacted. She was scared. They might have heard about the disease, how it was killing children in Africa, but they never expected to be nursing a malaria patient in their house.

We drove to Førde hospital. The local doctors never expected to deal with a malaria patient either. They had no idea what to do. They asked whether the disease was contagious and whether they should quarantine me. I told them to give me chloroquine, the most widely distributed malaria drug in Sierra Leone, but they had no idea what I was talking about. I realized that I was not getting anywhere with my explanation, so I asked if any of them had a friend in Germany who was a doctor. One of them knew some physicians in Germany. I had met many German doctors in Sierra Leone, and I assumed they would know about malaria.

By the time I was officially admitted and given a bed, my fever had gone down and I appeared well. However, I knew that if I wasn't treated before the next attack, it would be more dangerous. The second wave of a malaria attack usually includes vomiting, loss of appetite, and serious fatigue. Fortunately, the doctors returned with the news that a German friend had suggested a certain drug. It was one they did not have, but they had something closely related. I took the pills. The doctors visited me from time to time to chat about malaria. I told them about its agent of transmission—the female anopheles mosquito. When Desiree came to pick me up a few days later, she asked the doctor whether I was well enough to go home. The doctor replied that unless I loved Norwegian meatballs, which were a regular option on the hospital menu, there was no reason to stay. Desiree was relieved, and we drove home, talking about malaria.

I spent the rest of my time in Sande helping Desiree with her quilt business. I was responsible for folding and packaging purchased fabrics. I was not a stranger to handling fabrics. My mother is a seamstress, and I used to spend time with her, ironing, folding, and organizing fabrics. The time I spent with Desiree gave us the chance to talk about my life and the things I wished to do. She knew I was quiet and shy, so she asked small questions in order to gradually derive a full story out of me. "Have you ever had a girlfriend?" she asked. "Is she in Flekke or in Sierra Leone?" "Where is your mother now?" "So Joseph, do you need anything?"

We took a weekend off to visit Wenche and Sveinung at their summerhouse in Atløy. I love the outdoor beauty of Norway in the summer—fjords penetrating mountain ranges beneath the clear sky of long evenings. Sometimes twelve a.m. looked like twelve p.m. Most RCNUWC students never saw the beauty of Norway in the summer. School closes in May, when the sun begins to shine and the glaciers on the mountains start to melt. I was glad to be in Norway with so much free time. Desiree and Wenche stayed home while the rest of us went fishing in the sea. Inge loves to fish and is determined to return from each expedition with a salmon. Every time we drove to Førde, he stopped a few times to look in the fjord for signs of salmon. Each time he showed me a salmon he caught I joked that he bought it from the local supermarket. He was very excited to be on an island where he could fish all day. I simply enjoyed the luxury of free time and pleasant company.

We spent time on the island relaxing, eating, and drinking. I used the opportunity to update Inge and Desiree on my visa affairs. Desiree was very optimistic that the obstacle to my visa application would stay in Norway when I returned to Sierra Leone; otherwise, she said with her normal optimistic outlook, we could always work something out.

"Even if it is a matter of sending you some money to go to school in Sierra Leone, Inge and I can do that . . . right, Inge?" When Desiree speaks like this, Inge only smiles. Sometimes he adds a joke: "Only if Joseph agrees to babysit, eat a slice of *brun ost* every morning, and cook for us for a year."

I jokingly accepted Inge's terms, but warned him to make sure that his doctor inspected every meal I made before he ate it. We laughed and continued the feast, taking everything lightly. Inge enjoyed chuckling at my love for all Norwegian foods with the exception of *brun ost*, brown cheese. A *brun ost* TV commercial showed that one could not possibly master a Norwegian accent without eating the cheese. Some years later, I would find myself sitting in my American dorm room craving *brun ost*.

Shortly after returning from Atløy, we traveled to Fredrikstad, south of Oslo, for a few days. Fredrikstad is by the Glåma River, but there was no boat for Inge to go fishing. I swam with Elias and Anna Kamilla, who never got tired of playing in water. Everyone complained about the burning sunshine, but I was just beginning to feel at home. Most of the people I met during the Norwegian winters teased me for choosing the "wrong" country, but now I laughed whenever Desiree and Inge complained about getting burned in the sun. I sweat like everyone else, but where I'm from, one is happier drenched in sweat than frozen.

We returned to Sande just before it was time for me to go back to Sierra Leone. Desiree and Inge took me shopping for the trip. Whenever we went out to eat, Desiree recommended American food because she thought I should start getting used to eating it.

We usually ended up with burgers and sandwiches. We celebrated my departure by going to the Hørgeland Recreational Center at RCNUWC to swim and dine with Desiree's mother, who lives close to Flekke. The imminence of my departure made me a little sad, but as usual I tried to keep myself in the moment. I left Sande at the end of August and took a bus to Oslo, where I had a connecting flight to Belgium. I had a six-hour nighttime layover at Oslo International Airport. I was overwhelmed with sadness, so I simply stayed in the airport until my departure time.

SN Brussels was one of the few European airlines still flying to Sierra Leone after the end of the civil war. The flight to Sierra Leone was never full in August, because few West Africans return home at that time of year unless it's for business. Most go home in December for Christmas and New Year's celebrations. Others are satisfied with staying in the West to send remittances home to relatives, avoiding visa problems and the exorbitant flight cost altogether. The advantage of traveling in August is that I had three seats to myself, and there were fewer hustlers at the airport when I arrived. Most unemployed youths go to the airport in December to welcome the Just Comes with hopes of getting some change from their brothers and sisters from Europe and America. The struggle for survival in Sierra Leone can be seen in the eyes of the young people at the airport, hoping that someday one of the planes will take them to Amaika.

I joined my compatriots in the dream of going to Amaika. Though my chances were higher, I still feared that we were all in the same predicament. I had a full scholarship to study in the U.S., but without a visa I could no longer leave Sierra Leone for either the U.S. or Europe. The situation reminded me of my first voyage to Norway. But if the journey to the U.S. was anything similar to my trip to Norway, then everything would be just fine. All I needed was hope. But for the moment, I was happy to be home again.

CHAPTER 7

In life, the dead matter only to the living. So make your mark on those who will remember you.

When I arrived in Freetown in August 2004, my only goal was another attempt to obtain a U.S. visa. I love my country and it was wonderful to be back, but I was eager to pursue my education in America. I emerged from Sierra Leone like a germinating seed in a dry soil, painfully penetrating the wreckage of war. Sierra Leone is the source of my identity, my strength, and my pride. But it has undergone drastic changes, and my place in it had changed, too. I was a Just Come to the youths, a Santa Claus to the impoverished children I had served for the two years I was in Norway. When I'd left Sierra Leone in 2002, it had lain in ruin from a decade of civil war. Many children had had their limbs chopped off, others had been raped, some had lost their entire families. I launched SAFUGE in Norway to provide clothing, education, and medical assistance to children affected by the war in Sierra Leone. But I returned from Norway as a Westerner, an elite in a land of despair. No one's day would be ruined by my visa problems in a country where people still survived minute to minute. I had to pretend that everything was all right and life was beautiful. What could a boy coming from one of the richest countries in the world to the poorest possibly complain about? I would be mocking my people. So like all strugglers in Sierra Leone, *je fais semblant d'être content*. I pretend to be happy.

When I was a student at Sierra Leone Grammar School (SLGS) at the end of the 1990s, the war was going on, and the whole country was desperate. I lived with my uncle, Sahr Joseph Tolno, my mother's older brother, who had nothing but an old étage to shelter me and his family of six. Every morning, I walked up the hill behind our house to SLGS, the most prestigious high school in Sierra Leone. Sometimes I went without a proper meal for days. But the thought of my mother and siblings in a refugee camp in Guinea gave me the courage to overcome many obstacles. If there was ever a reason to stand firm, I had enough to stand for. My father had died unexpectedly when I was still a boy, without the customary transfer of family authority from father to son, but he had always admonished me to be there for my younger siblings and to use cautious judgment in settling family matters. Whenever a family dispute reached my father's personal court of arbitration, it was bound to end there. He established a reputation for unbiased and fair judgment, which made his rulings final. Those who delayed in paying their fines—or in granting forgiveness—often avoided contact with my father until they finally fulfilled his judgment. It was always entertaining to watch family members sneak out through the back door upon hearing my father's voice.

My father was a teacher who believed in teaching by example, which meant that as his older son, I was often the only pupil for his lessons on duty to family. I was usually chastised for the misconduct of my younger siblings and sometimes held solely responsible for our collective mischief. When my brother Francis forced me into a fight, I also suffered the heavy end of my father's whip, because in his judgment an older brother should know better. As if with the awareness that he was going to die early, my father trained me to take his place as head of our family. (Perhaps that's why my younger sister calls me "father.") I was learning to maintain order in his absence and to assume responsibility for the misconduct of my younger siblings when I failed to instill discipline. He taught me that the head of a family must always be the first to sacrifice for the family. There is a Sierra Leonean saying that there is no bad forest in which to throw away a bad child, but my father took it further to protect even the most wayward of relatives. If he had been a judge, he would have been an unwavering advocate for rehabilitation and reformation.

A room in our house in Pendembu was specifically reserved for emergency situations when someone might show up in the middle of the night looking for shelter. Maybe a family member needed help because another relative could no longer handle their behavior, or a random stranger's vehicle had broken down on the Pendembu highway. Some relatives came with rehearsed testimonies to sway my father to their side, but it was always interesting to observe my father's response: "There is no need for explanations now. Just eat some food and go to bed. I will send for your husband tomorrow, and we will resolve whatever it is together." Many of my father's friends still reminisce about the days when they used to run to Teacher, as he was known among friends and family, for quick advice on decisions they were about to make. Whenever I look back on that ominous day when my father departed and never returned, I am reminded of my duty to my mother and my siblings.

We escaped from Voinjama, Liberia, to Guinea in 1993 after Alhaji Kromah's United Liberation Movement of Liberia for Democracy (ULIMO-K) forces launched an attack against NPFL rebels occupying the city. My family fled without having any specific notion of where we were going. After a whole day of walking through bushes and abandoned villages, we arrived at the Liberian-Guinean border on the Makona (Moa) River. The soldiers guarding the Guinean side of the border denied us entry out of fear that we had rebels among us. After several hours of cross-river negotiations between the soldiers and refugees, the Caucasian missionaries in our group were let in. The missionaries helped negotiate for the refugees to be permitted across the border. My mother, who speaks multiple Sierra Leonean and Guinean languages, assisted with the discussions.

The border guards eventually said the women and children could cross, leaving the men behind, but they refused to provide a boat for us. Those who could swim made it across with a few strokes; others paid local fishermen whatever little money or few valuables they had to transport them. My mother had no money, so we got across by clinging to her shoulders as she walked across. She is tall, and the water level, luckily, was low because it was the dry season. As my two siblings and I clung tightly to her shoulders, I turned around a few times to look at my father, who stood on the bank of the river that separated us. I didn't understand what was happening, but as the men stood with their gazes fixed, like hawks, on their wives and children spread across the thick brown waters of the Makona River, I could tell something was not right. I never thought of not seeing my father again, either because my mother maintained absolute calm during the entire chaotic episode or because my mind was too young to know that I was being separated from my father potentially forever. Ever since our days in prison, my father never went anywhere without me, and I certainly did not think a mere river was barrier enough to keep us apart. My father and I had cheated death too many times and infiltrated the most impenetrable jungles; a river could not permanently divide us.

At the height of the recent Syrian refugee crisis, I was moved by news of refugees drowning while trying to reach safety in Europe, where they were rejected. I wrote a blog post, "Syrian Refugees Have Made Me Cry Tears I Never Shed for Myself," describing the similarities between our escape to Guinea and what Syrian refugees were facing in Europe. With a vivid image in my head of my family's struggles, I wrote, "Behind these people is war, and in front of them are other human beings who look at their supplicating faces and reject their pleas for refuge, a place to lay their heads away from the war at home." In the suffering of the mothers, I saw my own mother as she resiliently hauled us across an unfamiliar river under the hopeful gaze of her powerless husband. I called for the activation of the

1951 Refugee Convention to protect Syrian refugees, and I candidly addressed ordinary Europeans from the perspective of someone who had experienced a similar situation: "Under normal circumstances most people do not want to leave their country, the familiar safety of community, and the convenience of routine to knock at the door of others who do not want them there." I commended all Europeans who opened their doors to strangers and offered relief. Imitating the language of the beatitudes of Matthew, I called them the "guardians of the earth." In the early 1990s, Guinea, too, had its guardians of the earth, and they saved many refugees.

The Guinean border guards registered us and directed us up a hill to a small village called Gbetewaramie. It was one of the most chaotic African villages I have ever seen. Goats, sheep, pigs, chickens, and humans happily shared each other's space. The children had large bellies, and their entire bodies were covered in dust, probably accumulated over many months. The village was very uncomfortable, but we had nowhere else to go. We were homeless, lost, and wet. We marched in single file, instinctively, toward an empty hut that appeared to be a parliament of the various animal caucuses in the village. It took us several hours to empty the hut of the massive amount of feces the parliamentarians had deposited over the years. We claimed corners of the hut to rest for the night. It was the first time I saw Liberians, normally a chatty group of people, absolutely quiet. There were no questions or conversations, only the voices of hungry babies and random sighs from sympathetic mothers. I realized then how painful it is for a mother to listen to her crying child without the power to do anything about it.

"You kyan gave dat chad some tatay?"—can't you breast-feed that child?—a concerned person would ask.

"Ma sister, no moo milk in the tatay. Masef a nat eat whole day." My sister, there is no more breast milk. I haven't eaten all day either.

It could be that the panic I feel when I hear the voice of a crying child is rooted in those traumatizing days when children cried incessantly, when mothers shared infinitesimal amounts of food with their older children in order to be able to replenish some breast milk for their baby brother or sister. Most Liberians, like Sierra Leoneans and Guineans, believe that a child must eat before his or her parents, but the war created an atmosphere in which our beliefs were shattered by our struggle for survival. We became a lot more concerned with staying alive than with living.

My mother did not go to sleep after we settled in the hut. She went from door to door in the village, trying to find a better living space for us. My mother knew that sleeping in the open air with mosquitoes was not good for us children, especially Ben and Amie, ages two and eight at the time. She negotiated for a back room in a little mud house that leaned to one side and looked like it could fall at any moment. Still, it counted among the mansions of the village. My mother found wood, heated some water, bathed us, and put us to bed on a straw mattress that came with the room. Knowing that my father was out in the cold across the river, my mother didn't sleep that night.

Over the next several days, she spent most of her time on the bank of the river, translating messages from the United Nations High Commissioner for Refugees (UNHCR) and the local gendarmes and government officials concerning the men who were still across the river on Liberian soil, potentially exposed to tropical diseases and hostile rebels. Francis and I sometimes went along to help or just to be with her. The men hid at night to avoid a possible rebel attack and appeared during the day to yell messages to their wives across the river. We got excited whenever our father made it to the front of the crowd to wave at us. After days of negotiations, the men were allowed to cross into Guinea.

I was again reunited with my father. He was quieter and whistled more. Most of the men had become disheartened after their days in the jungle. It was not the first time that Guineans had offered such inhuman treatment to vulnerable refugees fleeing the conflagration of war. Before the war, Guineans, Sierra Leoneans, and Liberians lived in harmony and moved about freely within the Mano River Union, the same river basin that now divided us. Many Liberians were so displeased about the treatment of refugees in Guinea that they chose to die at home instead of face the humiliation of life as a refugee. This new phenomenon was spread by a slogan: "I born here I die here." Indeed, many stayed and died, but as patriots, not as rejected refugees.

My father had become one of those who were reluctant to escape. In Voinjama, we had waited until the rebels were too close and ended up fleeing under a hail of bullets. I was carrying on my head one of the few possessions we never left behind: my mother's Singer sewing machine. I had successfully crisscrossed through bullets, but I felt a bang above my head that swayed me to one side. I held tight, because the machine was a prized possession, and I also thought of how long Francis would laugh at me if I failed to save it. The force of the bullet strikes was so strong it swept me off my feet, but I held onto the machine as I fell to the ground. My father turned around, crouching, but could not reach me because the shooting had intensified. He gave me a look that reminded me that we had survived many battles, and this was not the end. And like a Hollywood hero who returns from near defeat to win a fight, I staggered to my feet, still carrying the battered Singer. It survived, and my mother transported it across the river. She later used it to repair what few clothes we had with us in Guinea.

Our hurried departure also caused us to forget to take another important item. My mother had set aside and dried a portion of fish from each of her fishing trips. She had packed the dried fish in a large carton and placed it under a bed. We only remembered the fish when were hungry on the first night of our escape.

It was during one of those fishing trips that Francis and I killed a crocodile. I have often told this story in a manner that portrays me as a heroic child version of the Crocodile Hunter. The unexaggerated report is that when the crocodile appeared, the women screamed and threw their fishing nets all over the place, which made it impossible for the crocodile to move away as fast as it might have, so Francis attacked it with a stick while I used my machete to finish the poor animal. Nearby rebels heard the commotion and came to the river. They slaughtered the crocodile and gave some of the meat to the women. Back then I felt tough defending my mother and her fishing mates from a crocodile, but the recollection of the incident saddens me sometimes. The poor animal!

We lived in the Guinean border village, with all its inconveniences, for several weeks before the UNHCR ordered us to move to a highway town called Tekoulo. The Tekoulo Refugee Camp was overcrowded by the time we got there, so we were put in a UNHCR truck and taken to Kondebadou Refugee Camp. We were very glad to leave the border village, even though we were uncertain about our next destination. Many African villages lag far behind modernity, with all its amenities, but the little border village lacked even the simplest inventions that make life a little better. There were no toilets or latrines, so we joined the army of people who made daily pilgrimages to the bush to answer the call of nature. In the bush latrine, even before one was done with his or her affair, sometimes a pig or a dog came by and quietly cleared the matter. My siblings and I enjoyed a great deal of laughter about the entire situation.

Kondebadou was a better camp. We were placed in temporary mud shelters with UNHCR tarpaulin roofs. We were officially registered as refugees and given food ration cards. Every month we received a small ration of cornmeal, beans, and a few liters of oil. Life improved a bit, but living conditions overall remained terrible. There was an outbreak of one disease after another. Children died of malnutrition, dysentery, cholera, and malaria. The cholera outbreak was particularly deadly. I remember the daily patrol of men in protective suits transporting corpses in black plastic body bags. The virus was spread by flies, but since we could do nothing about the filth in our overcrowded camp, they continued to breed, increasing the chances of a massive deadly outbreak. I had diarrhea a few times, but I never told my mother because I didn't want to worry her.

The food rations were never served on time, or they were too little for most families. They were issued on a monthly basis, but the food was hardly enough to last a week. The supply was particularly meager for families with no children. Many childless families paid kids like me to register as their children under fictitious names; sometimes we were recruited by multiple families at a time. The only requirements were a change of clothes and confidence. Occasionally children were disqualified because they forgot their new names. No matter how many appearances I made in a day, I remained confident, and I never forgot my new name.

The International Rescue Committee (IRC) established a primary school to keep children busy. The Red Cross constructed cesspit latrines and water wells to mitigate the spread of waterborne diseases. We buried many dead people, and some days we had no food to eat, but the diseases passed and Kondebadou became our new home.

After months in Kondebadou, my father moved to Gueckedou to teach at a bigger IRC refugee school. His plan was to come back for us as soon as he found a job. He was quite fortunate because former colleagues of his, some of whom had also been with us in prison, were established teachers at the refugee schools in Gueckedou. They quickly found him a placement at Bambo Refugee School. He taught for several weeks, and then one day he collapsed during a lesson. He was rushed to the Macenta Kura Hospital in Gueckedou, but nothing could keep him alive.

When a messenger with news of my father arrived in Kondebadou from Gueckedou to fetch my mother, our whole family was on a mountainside on the outskirts of town, breaking rocks for money.

We were contracted by a businessman who was building a store in Gueckedou to break boulders into pebbles. It was hard manual labor that paid very little money. A wheelbarrow of broken pebbles earned us around seven hundred Guinean francs (the equivalent of a few American cents), but we were fortunate to have five strong people on our team: my mother, Francis, Sisi Jeneba, my cousin Brima, and me. We spent our mornings breaking rocks, and in the afternoon my mother released all the children to go to school. On Wednesdays, Kondebadou market day, my mother made small plastic sachets of fried plantain that Francis, Brima, and I sold at the market. My mother had promised to buy us nice presents at the end of the rock-breaking season.

Without revealing to us children the full details of my father's fate, my mother accompanied the messenger to Gueckedou. I did not suspect that my father had died until she came back a few days later, wearing her black dress for the customary one-year period of mourning. She wailed, over and over, "Teecha ya nyaloi, nya yakpe geloi!" Teacher has departed without me, I am left alone!

I had no tears to cry with. I was angry—with God, the rebels, everything, and with my father, too. Why did he die? The next time I saw my father was in a photograph of his body, wrapped in white linen, ready to be buried.

My mother's Guinean relatives had been with my father when he died, and knowing that Kaifala is a Muslim name, they made arrangements for interment at a Muslim cemetery without being aware that my father was Catholic. My mother later turned down a proposal from my father's friends to exhume his body for reburial at a Christian cemetery, stating that fate had made it possible for him to be buried with Muslims, the faith of Mama Jeneba. My mother informed Francis and me about her decision, and we nodded in support. The fact of the matter is that my family never distinguishes between the two religions. We are all children of Adam, and God is God. My father would have said, "What difference does it make?

The man is dead." Whenever people rambled about an irrelevant aspect of an unchangeable situation, he would say, "The man died in a fire and you are wondering what happened to his beautiful beard."

I am the only one among my father's four children who got to know him a little. The only profession he enjoyed was teaching, and that is what he was determined to do with his life. Most people who knew my father call him Teacher even today. He valued education and freedom not only for his children, but for *all* children. His principles made him very charismatic among local youths in the Upper Bambara chiefdom of Kailahun district.

My father never said much, but he was known among his peers for his wisdom. During our time in detention in Liberia, he tried hard to minimize his inner struggles. For my sake, he couldn't give up. Every day, he promised me a bright future and kept me hopeful. At times he teased me about missing my siblings, but I realized that he missed them as much as I did. During our long walk from Liberia to Sierra Leone, he whistled songs or biblical hymns. I think it was a way of preventing himself from falling into deep thoughts, or maybe he was thinking of better days ahead. The song I remember most is "What Kind of Man Is Jesus?" which he also whistled during our fishing trips, when Liberia was still a peaceful country. I used to stand by his side along the banks of the St. John or Lofa river and listen as he endlessly whistled, while catfish and tilapia nibbled on our baited hooks. During one of those trips we went to a river that meandered through a sugarcane plantation that belonged to a rum distillery. An old planter gave me permission to eat as many canes as I wished. My father paid me no mind while I consumed a massive number of canes. I ate as many as my belly could hold, and then I passed out in the field. My father thought I was only sleeping, but the old man told him that I was wasted on cane juice. I was drowsy and weak, so the old man offered us a ride back to Voinjama in his truck.

My father had hoped that the war would end and he would teach again. But when we had to flee the war in Liberia a second time, he began to lose hope. His wonderful sense of humor diminished, and life weighed heavily on him. After years of physical and internal pain, he had hoped to rest in the refugee camp in Guinea. But death came for him too soon and left us without a father.

To be a man is not easy, indeed.

CHAPTER 8

*In times of anguish we must stay calm
and remember the good in our lives.*

It had been more than a month since my father died. My mother returned to Kondebadou to take us to Gueckedou for the fortieth-day memorial service. What little joy was left in my heart after years of escaping death was gone. My father, the legend of my family, was dead. My father and his mother, my two best friends, had died in my absence. Even though neither death was of their doing, I felt a dose of betrayal. There was no end-of-life transfer of hereditary knowledge from father to son, no ancient wisdom from grandmother to grandson, no final muttering of inaudible words and squeezing of hands, only dreadful news of their sudden deaths. I was traumatized, but I was sorry for my mother, whose pain I felt more than my own. She had been deeply in love with those two. Mothers-in-law are unpopular in many marriages, but my mother and my grandmother became inseparable friends. They had begun their relationship with an equal measure of jealousy and catfights, but they soon realized that they loved the same man, and that was that: the wife and the mother-in-law became friends. They were so close that people thought my mother was my grandmother's biological daughter.

My father's fortieth-day memorial brought together Sierra Leonean and Liberian refugees in Gueckedou. After a Catholic mass, a memorial reception was held at the Sandouno family compound in Macenta Kura, behind the very hospital where my father had breathed his last breath. The Sandounos and Tolnos—my mother's relatives—are cousins, so my mother was offered a room in one of the houses on the compound. Both families trace their origins to Tomadou village in Guinea, Foya in Liberia, and Koindu in Sierra Leone. My mother's older sister, Angeline Sandouno (Mama Yawa), who resides in Conakry, came to help her sister give my father a fitting memorial. Mama Yawa and her husband, Dr. Saa Dimeo Sandouno, purchased food and drinks for the vigil. Sisi Jeneba, who had left us in Kondebadou Refugee Camp to be reunited with her husband in Fangamadou Refugee Camp, came too. She was rather distraught by the loss of her favorite uncle.

Funeral rites are important to both Mende and Kissi people. My father's colleagues and friends gathered to give him a memorial befitting a brother, a friend, and an endearing teacher. The eulogies made my mother cry. In his short life, my father made a spectrum of friends, from orphans to priests and imams. Many of his friends who had escaped to Guinea came together to celebrate his life. The Guinean side of my mother's family also sent representatives to make sure their in-law received a dignified funeral. It is a part of Kissi culture to always treat a man who marries one's sister with dignity and respect. Patrick and Emmanuel Kailie, our family friends from Liberia, who had revived their cultural dance group in Gueckedou, provided a night of entertainment. There were prayers, songs, dances, and speeches glorifying my father. There was abundant food and drink for the guests. We ate and had a joyful but somber time together, reminiscing on my father's life. Teacher was dead, but his friends were happy that he'd lived. I don't know what I felt.

When the memorial was over and guests had returned to their homes, we were left to grapple with a future without my father. My mother was distressed, and it seemed that a part of her had died with her husband. She no longer laughed as loudly as she used to; instead, she cried regularly. Finda Marie, my mother's Guinean cousin, volunteered to live with us until my mother recovered from her grief. Finda Marie spoke French, Kissi, and Mandingo, which helped Francis and me improve our skills in those languages. As children, we acquired the new languages faster than Finda Marie could learn English or Krio. She spoke Kissi to us, and we learned Mandingo from the children of our neighbors. We experienced no major communication difficulties with Finda Marie, except when one day I entered a room and found her screaming at Francis, who for some reason was under a bed and refusing to come out.

"Francis, Francis, comot de bot!"

What she meant to say in Krio was "Francis, Francis, comot under di bed"—come out from underneath the bed. Francis adamantly refused, and Finda Marie kept repeating her newly invented Krio phrase. It was the most hilarious moment of our time together. When I saw Finda Marie years later, the first thing she said to me, smiling, was "Comot de bot." She spoke fluent Krio by then.

We lived in Macenta Kura for at least six months. Francis and I spent our days playing with the local Mandingo children. My mother was happy about our new friendships with them, because our Mende lineage extends to the Mandingo of Guinea. The Kaifala are descendants of the Camara of Guinea, and my mother always tries to bring us closer to our Mandingo and Kissi heritage. My younger sister Amie is the only child who bears our ancestral name, Camara, because Guineans use an ancestral name instead of the father's last name, as is the custom in Sierra Leone. The name Kaifala is a first name in Guinea. When Mama Yawa was leaving Gueckedou after my father's memorial, she took Amie with her as a way of assisting her widowed sister. Amie could not be enrolled in school as Amie Kaifala, so she became the proud bearer of our Camara last name. She later added a hyphenated Kaifala, which I can only interpret as her way of honoring our beloved father. I sometimes believe that by growing up apart from me, Francis, and Hawa, Amie felt left out.

Our mother was still in emotional pain, but Francis and I quickly assimilated into the Macenta Kura environment. During the day we walked around the neighborhood looking for suitable swamps to fish. Macenta Kura means New Macenta, and this brand-new Mandingo neighborhood was constructed on the edges of swamps. There were few fish in the swamps, but there were abundant *todi seng jangs*, long-legged frogs, which require a different fishing technique that we learned from our Mandingo friends. Since these amphibians mostly get their food from above water, we had to make our baited hooks hop like grasshoppers instead of letting them sink below water. The leaping bait enticed the frogs out of hiding. We had to be as swift as the frogs, because they only bite bait that is in motion.

We spent our days fishing or playing soccer, wandering between Hérémakono (which means "waiting for happiness"), Solondoni, and Macenta Kura neighborhoods. We returned home in the evening only to eat and bathe. Some days we spared an hour or two to play with Finda Marie before visiting our friends. Gueckedou was safe, and we were allowed to roam freely at any time of the day. Every night, children assembled in the living room of our Mandingo neighbors to watch African music videos and Bollywood movies. I was not a fan of Bollywood movies, but other children were. They memorized Indian songs and sometimes dialogues from the films, too. The plots of Bollywood movies are straightforward, and we followed them pretty easily. I sat through the movies, but my interest was in African music videos. Some of my favorite artists were Pepe Kalle, Sam Fan Thomas, Kanda Bongo Man, Aurlus Mabele, Diblo Dibala, Papa Wemba, Koffi Olomide, and Yondo Sister. My father listened only to reggae, jazz, and country, so I knew little about African pop music before moving to Gueckedou; that is when I fell in love with Yondo Sister.

Yondo Sister is one of the best soukous dancers. She is a non-conformist who may have been one of my earliest introductions to feminism. However, it was Freddy Meiway and his *zoblazo zouké* dance that lit the dance floor for children. The adults enjoyed Diblo Dibala and his band, Loketo, which had Aurlus Mabele as vocalist. The band introduced a faster form of soukous known as *loketo*, which means "hips." Men and women jiggled their hips to *loketo* as if they were possessed by trembling spirits. Even in the conservative Guinean society, women were permitted to spin their bottoms to *loketo* with dutiful precision. Wole Soyinka has stated that African women take their femininity for granted just as much as African males do their masculinity. Although the Islamic patriarchy in Guinea placed many restrictions on women in other areas of public life, it was usually lenient on the expression of femininity through music and dance. Radio Télévision Guinéenne (RTG) broadcast a nightly music-video program called *Parade*, which was watched by most households with a television. These days, I am flabbergasted by the self-appointed con- stables of African women's fashion and body image. These "lingerie inspectors" perambulate the public sphere in many African countries in tight pants, wearing *bonjour-la-terre-au-revoir-le-ciel* (long shoes with the toe pointing upward), measuring the lengths of women's skirts, with support from the clergy, clerics, and political opportunists.

In 1995, we moved to Bambo, a neighborhood located at the edge of Gueckedou and on the road to Macenta. My aunt Emilia, who was in France, had purchased a house for her parents, who had also escaped to Guinea from Sierra Leone. My grandmother Don Kona offered my mother a room. Grandma Kona is a Sandouno, and her late husband, Vandy, was a Tonguino. The Tonguino are descendants of Kai Londo, the Kissi chief who defeated Ndawa and founded Kailahun, the capital of Kissi Tongi Chiefdom, Kaila- hun district, Sierra Leone. The house Auntie Emilia bought was occupied by several family members, including my Aunt Hawa and her husband, Kabba; my cousins Musa, Christiana, and Keifa; and several extended family members. The boys occupied a room in a three-bedroom apartment behind the main house. My uncle, Mohamed Lord Vandy Tongi, or My Lord, as his students called him, occupied one of the rooms in the backyard apartment. My

Lord was born with a deformity that made his head disproportionately large in relation to his body. However, his huge head came with a bundle of intelligence and a beautiful mind that made him an admired teacher.

Legend had it that My Lord had memorized a dictionary when he was a high school student. He was an utterly intelligent man and a logophile, but I never believed that he'd memorized a complete dictionary. He was, however, a grammarian. He taught secondary-school English grammar and literature. He was the only teacher I have ever met who taught works of Shakespeare without a book in hand. He knew most of Shakespeare by heart and would recite dialogues from the plays verbatim. The same skill applied to the African literature he taught. His favorites were Ngugi Wa Thiongo, Chinua Achebe, Wole Soyinka, and African poets such as David Diop, John Pepper Clark, and Leopold Sedar Senghor. He would walk to class empty-handed and teach the material as if there were a teleprompter in his view. He would cite the chapter and quote the relevant material, and his baffled refugee students would sometimes irresistibly break into chants of admiration: "My Lord, My Lord, My Lord!"

My Lord had no child, so he informally adopted his sisters' children. He was the kind of uncle who told you why you were wrong and how to avoid repeating the same mistake without resorting to the African method, the whip. He assigned special roles to each of us, which we performed with delight. He entrusted Francis with reheating his leftover food in the morning. My cousin Musa was responsible for his laundry and transporting his materials to and from school. I was his designated secretary. When I was promoted to the seventh grade, he began to train me in making lesson plans, creating summaries of his lessons, and grading multiple-choice and short-answer English and literature tests. These responsibilities meant that I had to read and remember the materials, which subsequently placed me above my grade in school. I excelled in my classes and received double promotions. I started school in the fifth grade at

Bambo Refugee School, and at the end of the year I received a double promotion to the seventh grade at the Carrière Refugee School, hosted at a Guinean school named in honor of the Yugoslav leader Josip Broz Tito. Tito was a founding member of the Non-Aligned Movement, which included many newly independent African countries. I did my eighth grade at Carrière and received another double promotion, which took me to Kangoh Refugee High School. My Lord taught at all three refugee schools; therefore, Musa had no reprieve from transporting his bag, nor I from my secretarial job.

My mother was doing well a year after my father's death. She purchased a new Singer and slowly returned to sewing. She is happier when unfolding new fabrics, ironing, marking and cutting dress patterns, and pedaling threads across shapes. We celebrated my father's one-year memorial at church, but my mother would not stop wearing black. She continued to mourn my father despite concerns from family members and friends who recommended she find a husband to help her take care of her children. My mother did not yield, and for years she wore black in memory of her husband, my father, our beloved teacher. Francis was doing well in school too, and my sister Hawa joined us from Fangamadou Refugee Camp.

I missed my father and Mama Jeneba, but life acquired some normality in Gueckedou. Refugee life is what Raphael Lempkin described as a "permanent impermanence." Its permanence was based on the fact that we had no idea when the war would be over or whether we would ever return home. The impermanence rested on a constant reminder from the many relief organizations that Guinea was not home. Between permanence and impermanence, the life of a refugee hangs on uncertainty. When I was a student at RCNUWC, the attitude of one of my second-year roommates always reminded me of the permanent impermanence of life as a refugee. He placed his suitcase in the middle of the room on the first day and never fully unpacked, because he was constantly looking forward to going home.

Refugees had their own government and departments. The executive branch of refugee life and welfare was UNHCR, which governed every aspect of our existence. The two popular offices of UNHCR in Gueckedou were Protection and Resettlement. The Protection office was a judicial body that both intervened when refugees were accused of contravening Guinean law and settled refugee palaver. The Resettlement office was responsible for vetting refugees who qualified for asylum or resettlement elsewhere, mostly in the U.S. and Europe. The World Food Programme (WFP) was responsible for food and sanitary supplies. WFP provided monthly rations of bulgur, cornmeal, vegetable oil, and sometimes bars of soap. Even though these supplies were barely sufficient for a week or two, we could not have survived without them.

IRC held the role of Ministry of Education in the refugee administration. It provided primary, secondary, technical, and tertiary education to refugees. The organization also provided scholarships to academically meritorious students to study in the U.S., Europe, or Australia. I dreamed of receiving one of those IRC international scholarships. The Red Cross held the refugee health portfolio, and UNICEF ensured that children were healthy and got adequate playtime. UNICEF also collaborated with IRC to provide school supplies to refugee students at the beginning of every semester. Other subsidiary international agencies, such as Catholic Relief Services, Action Against Hunger, Concern International, the German Society for International Collaboration (then GTZ, now GIZ), and so forth, played vital roles in our survival as refugees. A savvy refugee knew all the organizations, what they did, and what time of the month to visit their offices.

Even children learned how to navigate the system. We embraced every new NGO or program. We joined debate clubs, drama clubs, dance troupes, scouting, and various community-service projects. We participated in these activities not because we were particularly interested in the various schemes, but because many of the organizations provided meals and certificates of completion. The certificates helped us enroll in other programs. Francis accumulated quite a few certificates before he left Gueckedou. I am versatile in many things today because of training I received from programs for refugee children. When I was in the tenth grade at Kangoh Refugee High, I wrote plays for a health club established by IRC to teach students about sexually transmitted diseases. I memorized the official health manual and wrote plays that were performed at Kangoh and Bambo Refugee Schools. Under the supervision of one of my teachers, Mr. Foh, we created a drama club at Kangoh Refugee High and performed plays such as *The Gods Are Not to Blame*, by Ola Rotimi, and *The Incorruptible Judge*, by Olu Olagoke. I loved *The Gods Are Not to Blame*, which is an African version of Sophocles' *Oedipus Rex*. I acted various parts in the play, but my main role was as Baba Fakunle, the blind soothsayer who reveals that King Odewale has killed his father and is married to his mother. Baba Fakunle is Tiresias in *Oedipus*.

Both plays raised questions in my mind about predeterminism—the idea that one's destiny is inevitable. The gods willed that Odewale would kill his father and marry his mother. There was nothing he could have done to evade his destiny. An attempt to sacrifice him when he was a baby had failed, and his own effort to escape only led him to fulfill the will of the gods. If Odewale could not escape his duty as assigned by the gods, then were the gods to blame for his misfortune? Are we endowed with free will, or are we simply here to accomplish individually assigned divine missions? The two plays center on the idea that mere mortals may try but cannot defy divine plans. When Odewale discovered his destiny as a prince of Ijekun, he asked the Ifa priest what he could do to avoid his fate. A voice answered, "Nothing. To run away would be foolish. The snail may try, but it cannot cast off its shell."

Odewale could have stayed and avoided his destiny, but that was in fact the bait that drove him to his downfall. The life of King Odewale was a manifestation of the parable "Death in Tehran": A man encountered Death, who threatened him. He asked his master to borrow his fastest horse so he could flee to Tehran by day's end. The master granted his request, and off went the servant. The master later encountered Death and asked why he had threatened his servant. Death responded, "I did not threaten him. I was only surprised to find him still here when I planned to meet him tonight in Tehran." Tiresias in *Oedipus* put it succinctly: "Terrible is knowledge to a man whom knowledge profits not."

Whether there is a god or not, I could not live life believing that I am a mere pawn in a divine game. To live a predetermined life means to squarely elude responsibility for one's actions. I call this the Judas conundrum. Judas Iscariot was a disciple of Jesus who betrayed him with a kiss for the price of thirty pieces of silver. His betrayal led to Jesus' arrest and crucifixion. However, if Jesus was born to live and die in fulfillment of the scriptures, then Judas was a necessary accessory to a divine plan. Jesus was aware of the fact that Judas would be the one to betray him, which he could have prevented, but Judas, like Odewale and Oedipus, had been willed to give the dishonest kiss that would lead to Jesus' arrest. The question many Christian denominations grapple with is whether Judas deserves damnation or salvation. On the other hand, if our lives are not predetermined and we live by free will, then Odewale and Oedipus were victims of anger, poor judgment, misunderstanding, and other human frailties. Judas was a thief, and those kings were victims of their own bad temperaments.

In spite of the difficulties of life as a refugee, I excelled in school. In addition to double promotions, I received many academic awards and won several quiz competitions. In the eighth grade, I led my team to victory against twelfth graders in a spelling bee championship. The contest ended in a tie after a full round, then our opponents misspelled their bonus word. Students from many local refugee schools attended the event, which was held on the field at Carrière Refugee

School to accommodate all attendees. I remember the silence and the sudden gush of cool breeze as the moderator explained that because our opponents had missed their bonus point, my team would win the championship if we spelled the next word correctly. I was the contestant who would spell the word aloud, although I was permitted to consult with my teammates before answering. The master of ceremonies took his time explaining the rules while I listened carefully. He was a teacher who enjoyed the limelight, and he used the opportunity to make a winding statement about the rules that was irrelevant to us, because we knew the rules. When he felt he had impressed those present with his verbosity, he got to the point.

"Dear contestant, your bonus word is *synonym*!"

I knew how to spell the word, but I was carrying the weight of my team and the support of our fans on my shoulders. A mistake would have been careless. The silence was broken by murmurs to the effect that My Lord's *pikin*—child—could never disappoint. I wrote the word down, took another look at it, and paused. I looked toward the faculty section and saw many of my father's former colleagues, who were now my teachers, smiling with confidence. I consulted my teammates and rose slowly from my chair. I did all this to heighten the suspense. Students in the front rows of the audience stood with me like congregants at a Catholic mass. Others climbed onto their chairs. There were pulls and pushes, swearing and sucking of teeth. No one wanted to miss the last dramatic moment of the contest.

Then there was silence. Impatient students continued to shove and elbow each other, but there was no more speaking. They were waiting for me, and I was enjoying the spotlight. As soon as I pronounced the final *m* and the excited moderator said "Correct," a crowd of supporters picked me up and raised me toward the sky. They ran around the field carrying me and singing victory songs until they were told to bring me back for the award ceremony. After the prizes were given, I was again lifted toward the sky, and the party continued until we were all exhausted. My Lord was proud of me. "That's my boy!" he told a group of teachers who stood around discussing the event. News of our championship victory spread throughout Gueckedou and to nearby refugee camps. I was humble and shy, but I smiled back at the girls.

I loved journalism, so I joined the Carrière High News Organ (CHINO). The twelfth-graders read the daily news at devotions, but they left the microphone and radio receiver to juniors during public celebrations. I enjoyed walking around with my microphone at public events and interviewing students. When I moved to Kangoh Refugee High, I joined the Kangoh High News Organ (K-HINO). My friend Porter and I sometimes read the morning news at devotions. I felt a level of pride whenever I read the introduction before the headlines: "This is Joseph Kaifala, and here is your news in brief."

One day, Porter and I were the news and also had to report the news. When I started at Kangoh Refugee High, WFP had just introduced school feeding. Each refugee student received a ticket for a daily plate of cornmeal and bean soup. The serving was so small that it did little to alleviate our hunger. Porter and I realized that the cooks were illiterate and could not distinguish the school stamp on a meal ticket. We simply obtained the same-color paper, cut it into identical shapes as the official ticket, and stamped the backs. It worked so well that we often had extra meal tickets to offer our friends. However, a jealous student discovered our fraudulent activity and reported it. We were caught and taken to the principal's office for punishment. The following morning, we had to read the news in which we reported on ourselves. The entire student body burst into laughter as Porter read the headline: "Two Students Caught with Counterfeit Meal Tickets." I giggled uncontrollably. The principal thought that reading the news about ourselves was sufficient humiliation and forgave us. My Lord was amused by the whole trick.

There were many refugee children and not enough schools. Therefore, each school had a morning session and an afternoon session. The younger grades attended in the morning and the older grades in the afternoon. I studied hard, even though I was always hungry. There were too many of us living in one refugee household, and there was never enough food. There were six boys, and we ate from the same bowl. Our dinner was never more than two or three handfuls. Sometimes, in our selfish attempts to eat more than each other, we *kapu*, scrimmaged the food. In the end, we only succeeded in wasting our meager meal. After a while, we came up with a solution of just partitioning the food. Since the portions were drawn by human hand without scientific measure, they were usually unequal, and the first person to pick a share always had more food. Therefore, dividing was an undesirable role, but being the one to pick first was coveted.

We invented a scheme that guaranteed some fairness. Our parents would never have allowed us to eat separately, so we came up with a solution that everyone could live with. Whoever was first to openly announce himself as "first to take" acquired the right to pick first. The last person assumed the role of divider. Since all six of us slept on the same straw mattress, it was always funny to hear an early riser tap another sleeper on the shoulder and announce, in a drowsy voice, "First to take." The now-awakened person would answer, "Second to take." It was often smarter to start whispering, "First to take" before waking someone up, because sometimes the sleeper would instead steal the spot and number one would end up second. Musa was the only one I ever woke up, and he never betrayed me. I got my first spot, and he settled for his second. The divider had to be fair in order not to end up with a disproportionately smaller portion. We no longer fought over our food, and we ate in peace, even if it was still insufficient for our hungry bellies. We also achieved a safeguard against Big Brima, an older uncle whose hands were larger than ours. Before our "first to take" scheme, he had always ended up with most of the food.

When we were too hungry to sleep, we ran covert missions in search of food. Our choice of food to raid depended on the season. Cassava and corn were easy targets. We sometimes raided neighborhood mango, avocado, and banana farms. One time, we raided a mango farm, but unfortunately the farmer had not yet gone home. The old man chased us and caught my cousin Tuku. She was a fast runner, but an unfortunate fall led to her capture. When the farmer realized that Tuku was just a child, he decided to scare her before letting her go. He said he would place her in a mini chicken coop and take her to town. The thought of getting shoved into a coop meant for fowls made Tuku scream hysterically. The farmer amused himself by repeating his intent to place Tuku in a coop every time she stopped crying. When he was satisfactorily amused, he let her go, but Tuku became the butt of the joke at home. Tuku is now a young woman, but we still tease her about her chicken coop incident.

Our easiest mission involved making honest purchases from a polygamous family that lived near us. All the wives—and there were almost a dozen of them—sold parched peanuts in small plastic sachets outside their compound. They lined up their peanut trays and returned to their chores. When we wanted a bag of peanuts, we simply yelled, "Tia!" and by the time they arrived for the transaction, we had stocked our pockets with a bag from each tray. It was what you may call ten for the price of one. The women never suspected us, and we never stopped taking advantage of the opportunity to obtain a few small sachets of nuts. From the look of things, the women were not in it for the profit. I suspect that the peanut trade was their only chance to be outside their polygamous compound at night. Apart from going out to purchase ingredients to cook for their family—and each wife cooked every day—they never left the compound. Their husband was a wealthy merchant who made enough money to marry many wives. Some of the wives already had one or two children.

We developed our own legitimate business as well. We discovered a wild berry—*dolokoh* in Mandingo—that was popular with children at a local private school. The students received school lunch, and most of them also brought food from home. They had no problem spending their lunch money on wild berries; if their parents had known, they would not have tolerated the behavior. We earned our own lunch money by selling the berries to the children against the wishes of the school's administrators, who often chased us away.

I developed a crush on a beautiful girl who was in the sixth grade at the private school. She always purchased dolokoh from me, but we never learned each other's names. She simply gave me whatever sum of money she had, smiled, and I emptied my pocket of dolokoh into her tender hands. Some days she brought no money to school and I gave her my dolokoh anyway. On Mondays, when she had more lunch money, she overpaid for whatever dolokoh I gave her. When I saw her downtown with her parents on Saturday or Sunday, she greeted me with her usual smile.

"Dolokoh ti ça va?" she would say.

"Oui, ça va!" I responded with a warm blush spreading across my dark cheeks. We continued our separate ways until we were together again behind her school to trade dolokoh, blushes, and smiles.

Francis made more money than I did selling dolokoh because he was good at climbing trees and could reach the farthest berries. I was always nervous when he climbed to the top of tall trees and placed himself on the smallest branches. One of the times I came closest to getting killed in Pendembu was when I refused to hand over to a group of rebels the coconuts Francis had struggled so hard to harvest. In the tall limbs of a coconut tree, he had competed with a huge snake to get to the nuts. As soon as the rebels—child soldiers—saw us with the coconuts, they approached us and told us to give them over. When I refused, one of them took a couple of steps backward and cocked his gun. Fortunately, another rebel who was standing nearby ordered him to stop. He had been one of the guards stationed at our prison in Voinjama. I tell this story to illustrate my belief that there is goodness in all of us that is sometimes subdued for alternate desires, but avails itself under the right circumstances. A child soldier who could have killed me in Liberia saved my life in Sierra Leone.

Our parents did not worry about our whereabouts as long as we did our assigned chores. Every morning I had to sweep the house or the yard. We took turns scrubbing the toilet. Cleaning the toilet was not a pleasant chore in a household of more than a dozen people, but we had to do it. We also fetched our drinking water from a spring three miles away. A group of us walked to the watering hole with our five-gallon containers every morning or night. During the dry season, the little stream provided water for Gueckedou and other surrounding villages.

Our other major chore was to fetch firewood. Every other Saturday, we went to Hundoni, a village about five miles away, to get wood. I enjoyed the trip to Hundoni because it was one of the few times we were together without adult supervision. It didn't matter how long we took, as long as we returned with wood. When we were in the forest near Hundoni, the only goal was to find the best wood; nothing else was significant. We joked, laughed, and played to the fullest. The jungle was thick enough to maintain the privacy of our chattering, and the sky was wide enough to spread the echo of our laughter. When we gathered the wood, each of us made a bundle he or she could carry without strain—although there was always a subtle competition among the boys about whose bundle was bigger. We walked home in a group and took breaks along the way.

Whenever we went wood-fetching, our parents made sure food was ready before we returned. Though our food ration was never commensurate with the size of our labor, we appreciated the gesture from our parents. We witnessed and understood what our parents sometimes had to go through to offer us one meal a day, so we never made childish requests or the sorts of irrational demands privileged children make of their parents. We were delighted when we received new shoes or uniforms. Our parents allowed us to play outside as much as we desired. The longer we were away from their sight, the less they had to worry about all the things they could not do for us. Whenever my brother and I nagged our mother with a request she could not fulfill, she responded in Kissi, "E cho ganda ma cho wella lae." I am squeezing, but it is not getting dried. We took the cue and dropped the matter, however meaningful it may have been to our unfortunate lives.

What occupied us more than anything else in those days was our football club. Many of the children in the Bambo neighborhood joined a club called Les Berets Rouges, the Red Berets. One of our players was a boy from a wealthy family whose father bought our red jerseys, footballs, and shoes. We had many talented players, including our goalkeeper René, a Soso boy who moved like a cat, and my cousin Sahr Kendema, who was a talented dribbler. I was not one of the skillful players who dribbled much, but I was great at precision passes and defense. I was also the team manager, who made sure all jerseys were returned clean and ready for our next match. The boy whose father was our team's financier was not good at accepting defeat. Sportsmanship was not his forte. Whenever we were down a couple of goals, he would instruct the players to pick up the ball, which was usually ours, and abandon the game. It was easier when we played at home, but away matches sometimes involved literally running away with our ball when the opposing team refused to let us quit the match.

My mother allowed me to participate in all these activities as long as they never interfered with schoolwork. I was usually ahead of my grade, and my teachers heaped praise on me whenever they saw my mother. I took seriously the task of assisting my uncle with his lesson plans and grading his students. Every year he taught *Weep Not, Child* or *Things Fall Apart* in addition to other literature. *Weep Not, Child* introduced me to colonialism and Africa's liberation struggles through the Kenyan experience. In those days, I thought like Njoroge. I saw education as my way out of poverty and as preparation to someday become a leader of my country. When I was a child, I noticed that adults were always trying to go to the U.S. or Europe, and good things came from those places, which placed the idea of white superiority in my head. It was from the barber in *Weep Not, Child* that I learned that whites, as he put it, "are not the gods we had thought them to be." It was my first experience with the demystification of the white race.

Things Fall Apart remains the best African literature I have ever read. The book is set in Nigeria, but the story is universally African. I developed great admiration for the tragic hero, Okonkwo, whose virtue was hindered by his hot temper. He lived an honorable life, but in the end his honor was his ruin. He was caught in the quagmire of culture, but his loyalty was with the gods, which is why he participated in the killing of his ward, Ikemefuna, even though a respected elder warned him against taking part in the ritual. Okonkwo's friend Obierika, who did not participate in the killing, said he did not disagree with the gods, but nor did they give specific instruction that he should be the one to execute their order. Such an excuse irritated Okonkwo because that is what his lazy father, Unoka, would have said. Most sons grow up emulating their fathers, but Okonkwo lived life in distinction from his father, who was an *agbala*—a man of no title. In spite of his achievements, Okonkwo was "a man whose *chi* [personal god] said nay despite his own affirmation."

When I later studied *Things Fall Apart* with Maria Teresa, or MT, my IB English teacher in Norway, she said I had the qualities of Okonkwo and began to call me Okonkwo. "Guys, doesn't the description of Okonkwo fit our own Joseph?" she said after reading any passage with a description of Okonkwo's personality. My classmates looked at her, often unconvinced. Some thought she was racist; I thought she was funny. There is no fiber of racism in MT's bones.

Things Fall Apart also provides a concise depiction of the early penetration of Christianity into African society. The struggle against the new religion became an unwinnable fight as more Africans abandoned their gods for the occupying deity, an intruding god. The title of the book conveys the chaos created by the new religion, but it is Obierika's reflection when he visits Okonkwo in exile for the last time that encapsulates the agony of the irreversible taint of Christianity on African cultures. I can still hear My Lord's voice as I heard it on countless occasions when he recited Obierika's words like poetry: "The white man is very clever. He came quietly and peaceably with his religion. We were amused by his foolishness and allowed him to stay. Now he has won our brothers, and our clan can no longer act like one. He has put a knife on the things that held us together and we have fallen apart."

I often thought that I would grow up and know all the books like My Lord. I listened intently as he explained the literary meaning and applicability of these words to contemporary society. As time passed, I began to understand literature without my uncle's assistance, and I developed the ability to make connections between what I read and my environment. Remembering literature became a delightful game I played with my uncle. He would quote a passage from a book we had both read, and I was expected to either quote the succeeding passage or another that complemented or contradicted his passage. We also played this game with poetry. My uncle recited a line, and I recited the next.

His favorite poem was "The Vultures" by David Diop. When I did well, he expressed his satisfaction with a wide smile that forced his mouth to extend across his large face. I can still hear the melancholy in his voice as he recited line thirteen: "You who knew all the books but knew not love." The line remains with me as an indictment of knowledge devoid of love.

Grammar School (second from left)

Grammar School Thanksgiving (second from right)

With fellow SLGS scouts

SLGS Thanksgiving parade

SLGS Penny day

With SLGS friends (right)

SLGS

SLGS Wall

SLGS Wall

SLGS Wall

Neighbor's cinema hall

Part 7 Andrew Street

Andrew Street kitchen

Andrew Street toilet when it fell after a heavy

Transportation between Guinea and Sierra Leone

Transportation between Guinea and Sierra Leone

My bed after we were evicted from Andrew street

Joseph & Older Sister Hawa

My mother Tewa Magdalene Kaifala
(right)

Tewa Magdalene Kaifala (left)

Ben M. Kaifala

My father Ben M. Kaifala & mother (middle)

Cover of my SLGS Exam ID

JK

JK (with my SLGS prefect
badge and ceremonial tie)

CHAPTER 9

Love, if it is love, must always come in full measure.

At the end of 1996, my cousin Musa received a message to report to the U.S. embassy in Conakry, Guinea, as soon as possible for a visa interview. I was sad to hear that my best friend was leaving, but, like everyone else, I was happy he was going to America, even if all I knew about America was whatever I had read in my geography and history books. Outside of my academic perceptions, America was a paradise, because that is what everyone said. Whatever America may truly have been, I knew that Musa would no longer scramble for food with us, and this was his chance to obtain a far better education. It also meant that I would have a "brother" in America—a reason for me to enter one of those glass phone booths at the post office to receive calls. In those days there were no cell phones or personal land lines in Gueckedou, so one went to the post office to make international calls. My neighbors would respect me when they heard that I had a relative in America. In those days, our America, the paradise, was made up of two states: New York and California. Musa was set to go to California.

The whole neighborhood knew that Musa was going to America. After news spread of his imminent departure, neighbors smiled at us when we walked to school. Those who were unsure about which of the two of us was Musa debated among themselves. Sometimes they got it right. The girls became even more flirtatious, and I enjoyed every bit of it. However, sadness consumed me whenever it occurred to me that soon I would be walking those long-distance roads by myself. Musa and I traveled at least six miles each way to and from school every day, but it felt like a stroll in the park because we did it together. We cracked jokes, shared snacks, and sometimes raced each other, but now Musa would soon be gone. I would walk alone, hungry and disinterested. Those few days before Musa departed, I oscillated between short bursts of thrill and anguish.

Auntie Hawa, Musa's mother, threw a farewell party for her son. She invited Musa's friends, classmates, teachers, and our whole neighborhood. Members of the Berets Rouges, our soccer team, were also invited. A trip to America was a great accomplishment. We gathered to congratulate Musa for receiving what most refugees dreamed of and spent years expecting from the UNHCR Resettlement Office: an invitation to America. Since this was a grand affair, we slaughtered a goat and cooked many large pots of *jollof* rice. Cooking was usually done at a fireplace made with three rocks placed in a triangular arrangement, but for such a grand farewell party, four enormous three-legged pots were required. Many crates of beer and soft drinks were purchased. My uncle Kabba, Auntie Hawa's husband, made a large barrel of alcoholic punch. It was one of the biggest parties Gueckedou had ever seen.

We wore our best clothes, and for a moment the only obstacle between our bellies and more food was limited space. One can never eat more than enough. The sound system was turned on, and we hit the dance floor. In most African societies, a party without dancing is incomplete. The adults danced and drank like tilapia. No matter how grand the event, if there is no music, it will always be the missing *je ne sais quoi*. One of my teachers ate and drank so much that he defecated on himself. Those of us who witnessed the poor man's bowel accident promised never to mention it in Gueckedou. He was perpetually kind to me after the incident, but I never forgot why.

We took pictures with Musa so that he would not forget us the moment we were out of sight. At one point we changed into our football jerseys and took a club photo with our departing not-too-shabby forward. My mother gave Musa some African attire to help him keep his origins in mind. I had a few extended family members in America, but I was more excited for Musa, because he was one of us, a refugee who had now received a chance to live a better life.

Musa, Francis, Keifa, and I were well known in Gueckedou. We were My Lord's *pikins* among the refugees. Other Gueckedou residents knew us as talented troublemakers. We used to walk around town both doing good and causing havoc. We were the kind of children everyone knew as good kids, but no one in his or her right mind would vouch for our next behavior. We had girlfriends in the neighborhood, and their fathers kept a wary eye on us. Most of our girlfriends were the cooks in their households, and they often made sure we had our share of the meal, sometimes the best of whatever they prepared. I dated a Kissi girl by the name of Finda. She was dark skinned and had beautiful white eyes. Finda lived with her older sister and the sister's husband, who worked for the United Nations. Finda and her younger brother did the cooking and household chores. Since Finda lived by the school where we sold dolokoh, we often visited her to pick up a large bowl of fried fish she had reserved for us. I was in love with Finda, but I often had to contend with her jealous younger brother, who jumped on me like a monkey every time I got close to his sister. Since we refused let him hang out with us, because his brother-in-law would never have allowed him to, he prevented me from kissing his sister.

Francis dated Janette, another beautiful Kissi girl who also lived with her sister and brother-in-law, a respected business tycoon in our neighborhood. Janette cooked for her family on weekends, when she was not in school. When she cooked, she sent us a huge bowl of rice, wrapped in beautiful cloths, like the adults did for their boyfriends. One day we made a collective blunder that could have led to trouble had her brother-in-law acted like other African parents. Janette used her brother-in-law's beautiful insulated bowls to bring us food. The following day, we walked past Janette's house on our way to go fishing. We were usually good at returning dishes, but that day we laughed our way out of the house, poking fun at each other, and forgot them.

We had been fishing for only a couple of hours when a little boy arrived to inform us that Janette's brother-in-law, who everyone knew as her father, was walking to our house with the little girl who had delivered the food there. Janette's brother-in-law was one of a few men who could order the police to arrest an individual, and it would be done immediately. This man was walking to our house. We stopped fishing to think about the possibility of jail time. We were afraid. We chose the path of avoidance and delayed our return home. We knew that whatever consequences awaited us, as long as we were out there by the riverside, no one could arrest us. I stood boldly on a log in the middle of the river, casting my line, while we discussed tactics and defenses, when suddenly someone screamed, "Snake!" I looked up and saw a huge snake advancing toward me with extreme speed. I had never seen a snake move that fast. I turned around to ask for a stick to kill the snake, but by the time I looked back, it was near my feet. My only choice was to jump over the snake and into the river. My swift plunge made my friends laugh and clap. The snake escaped, and I swam back to shore.

We walked home that evening, still analyzing our unknown fate at the hands of one of the wealthiest men in town. News of his visit to our compound had spread, as fast as rumors do in poor communities, and neighbors smiled at us with a sort of satisfaction as we passed them. Many of them had wanted to punish us for "chasing" their daughters around, but now a more powerful public figure was about to do the job for them. When we entered our compound, the adults were still discussing the visit of the wealthy man. My mother turned to my brother and me and asked whether our plan was to kill her by inviting trouble to her doorstep. My mother asked this question whenever the scrapes we got into in the streets followed us home. Francis and I stood sheepishly with nothing to say in our defense. We never had anything to say when our mother posed her guilt-infused questions. The food had been delicious, and we should have returned those bowls, but we had no intention of committing matricide by mischief. As for the "Catholic mother's guilt trip," it always induced the desired remorse in my brother and me.

It turned out that the wealthy man had visited our compound to make sure that his wife was not sending food to another man and Janette was not being exploited by an older man. He had walked right into our compound and told the little girl to lead him to the room where she picked up the dishes. He saw our room and realized we were a bunch of teenagers. He nodded to our nervous parents and walked away without saying a word. Janette, who had also been worried that her brother-in-law was going to arrest us, later told us that he had found her in the kitchen shivering. But instead of punishing her, he calmly told her that the next time she wanted to send food to her little boyfriends, she'd better use another bowl. We laughed about the incident for weeks and eventually befriended the wealthy man. He sometimes stopped his car and gave us money when he saw us walking to school. He later hired my mother to fill one of the highest positions in his company, even though he was aware that she was the least literate among those vying for the post.

Musa left Gueckedou for Conakry and eventually made his way to Freetown, where he waited for his visa. Things were not the same after Musa left, but I carried on doing well in school and helping My Lord with his lessons. After Musa left, I spent more time with My Lord. He became my close friend, and I never saw him angry until the day his father insulted him about the size of his head. My Lord was cognizant of his deformity and paid no mind to children who sometimes made fun of him in the streets, but one day an altercation between him and his father escalated to a point where his father looked at him from a distance and said in Kissi, "Boten ma boten nawoo!" Your head is as big as the head of a cow! My Lord launched himself at the old man, who was probably in his nineties. We did not know his age, but we knew that he was really, really old.

It was an intense fight. All the children tried to separate them, but both fighters were strong and angrier than we had ever seen them. Grandpa Vandy, who usually needed the support of a rotund wooden stick to walk, was standing upright. At one point he threw the walking stick at My Lord, and but for a good duck by my intellectual friend, there would have been a disastrous result. Luckily, he moved his head aside and the flying stick passed him to hit the flower bush that grew against the wall. The attacks and counterattacks continued until we managed to get My Lord outside the compound and seat the old man in his chair. They continued to throw verbal punches at one another, but further physical fighting was averted. When tempers had cooled, My Lord went on his usual promenade around town, and the old man went out to conduct his daily evangelism. Grandpa Vandy was a devoted Jehovah's Witness who never missed a day of preaching.

In 1997, Grandpa Vandy gave up and died. I had begun to notice that he was drawing near to the end of his life. The night before his death, I was studying late at night with the other children when we heard him crying. He was in pain. Our parents were sleeping, so we brewed some tea and helped him drink it. We stood around his bed until he was calm. We said nothing to each other because we were all thinking the same thing: our grandpa was dying. Christiana, my youngest cousin, felt Grandpa's pain, and she began to cry. She was not old enough to understand death, but it was evident that Grandpa Vandy, the independent old man, who unlike most men his age always did his own work, lay helpless.

We awoke the next morning to the weeping of Grandma Kona, and we realized that the inevitable had occurred. Our grandpa was no more. Because he was a devout Jehovah's Witness, his burial would have been simpler had he not also been a Kissi man from a reputable clan, Tongi. Gueckedou was far from Buedu, his home-town in Sierra Leone, but he had to be buried with the dignity of a Tongino. Another cause of delay was that he would not be buried until his oldest daughter, Auntie Emilia, arrived from Paris. He was washed, dressed, and laid in the living room, where his wife, Grandma Kona, slept beside him for days. Family members and friends who trickled in to mourn him also kept nights of vigil around his body. He was never taken to the mortuary, which may or may not have been operating anyway. Some of the children in the house were scared of the presence of a corpse, but death no longer had that effect on me.

It was agreed that Grandpa should be buried in the compound. It is a Kissi custom to bury the dead either at home or close to home. In this case, it was also pragmatic to bury Grandpa Vandy at home, so that his children could repatriate his body to Buedu when the war ended in Sierra Leone. A concrete tomb was constructed in a corner of the compound, with a "palaver hut" for small gatherings. A cow was slaughtered, and a copious amount of food was cooked for those who came to mourn. Grandma Kona's Guinean sisters and cous-ins came to mourn their in-law and console their sister. Relatives and friends originally from Buedu visited from surrounding refugee camps. Grandpa Vandy's funeral was planned according to Kissi tradition, but due respect was paid to his life as a staunch Jehovah's Witness. While everyone who knew him also knew that he would have wanted everything to conform to Kingdom Hall guidelines, a Kissi man is a Kissi man above everything else he may become.

Not long after Grandpa Vandy died, my mother obtained a temporary teaching job with the International Rescue Committee Vocational Training Center (IRC-VTC). She was hired to teach tailoring classes to refugee students. IRC-VTC was a major tertiary institution for refugee students. My brother and I were granted a scholarship to attend the institute while we were still in junior high.

We took French classes toward a professional certificate, which we both passed. I also took typing classes, but all we did most of the time was repeatedly type *ASDFJKL* and semicolon. The teacher was my father's former colleague in Liberia, so he called on me for every demonstration. In every class I ever took that was taught by someone who knew my father, it was only a day or two before all the students knew my name. "Kaifala this and Kaifala that." "Kaifala, stand up." "Kaifala, sit down." "Kaifala, tell us the answer." "Kaifala should know." It made me study hard to avoid embarrassment, but sometimes I just wanted to be invisible.

My mother is a professional seamstress, but she was not adequately literate to create the required lesson plans by herself. I quickly studied the sample manual and became her helper. One weekend every month, we worked on a tailoring lesson plan. I learned a lot of tailoring jargon, which my mother sometimes knew in French but not in English. I lost a great deal of playtime during lesson-plan weekends, and sometimes I got mad and my mother had to plead with me, but I was usually happy to help because I knew she needed it. The income from IRC-VTC contributed enormously to our lives. My brother and I now had new shoes and uniforms. Teaching and spending time with colleagues, even though most of them were my late father's friends, also diverted my mother's thoughts from my father, at least for some moments each day.

In May 1997, there was a military mutiny in Freetown, and the Armed Forces Revolutionary Council (AFRC), commanded by Major Johnny Paul Koroma, overthrew the government of Sierra Leone, headed by President Tejan Kabbah. We were all worried about Musa, who had gone to Freetown to await his U.S. visa. Fortunately, he was able to escape Freetown and return to Conakry, Guinea. President Kabbah also escaped to Conakry, and the AFRC soldiers took over the country. Musa would gather the strength to return to Gueckedou, a place he had already said good-bye to. We welcomed him as though he had never left, and he reenrolled in school. I was sad that Musa had not gone to America, but I was also happy that we were reunited, taking the same dusty shortcuts to Kangoh High School.

One of Musa's old classmates, Barry, sometimes walked with us. We befriended a new student, Moiwo, who also had escaped the Freetown coup d'état. One of my distant cousins, Elizabeth, another Freetown escapee, joined our group. The five of us were members of the renowned Kangoh High Drama Society, headed by a beloved teacher, Victor Foh. When we performed *The Gods Are Not to Blame*, Moiwo played King Odewale, Elizabeth was the understudy for Ojuola, Musa played Aderopo, and Barry was one of the chiefs. My friend Thomas George also played a chief. I felt a conflict of interest whenever My Lord assigned me to grade their exams, but they were all so smart that I never gave them grades they did not deserve. I have always had the makings of a fair-minded judge. My Lord knew that I would have had no qualms about failing my friends if they were stupid. I hold the view that school exams should present no surprises to those who study.

Musa was a little different when he returned from Freetown. He was a suave, confident city boy now. He knew the lyrics to American pop songs and had developed an interest in tennis. Although he did not play any tennis in Gueckedou, he followed all the tennis stars. He did not have to tell me that he was a big fan of Pete Sampras and Martina Hingis; his tennis stories always came back to spectacular games those two had won. I enjoyed the stories, but we had no television, so I had not seen a single professional tennis match. Still, Musa made me pay greater attention to those two names on Africa Sports News. Musa also came back a fan of Pato Banton, especially his song *Go Pato*, which he sang all the time.

Musa was still my brother and best friend, but he had improved at every social skill, including flirting with girls, a talent I lacked.

I was too serious. My new Ghanaian girlfriend, Gifty, and I barely talked to each other, and when we did, we fought. Gifty and I became lovers in the eighth grade when I volunteered to help write her class notes because she had a sweaty hand. Her hand looked like it was submerged in water whenever she squeezed a pen. I always copied my notes for Gifty—except when we were fighting, of course. She kept a small hand towel with her during exams to avoid ruining her papers with sweat. I found her sweaty hands, upper lip, and forehead rather cute. She had smooth, dark skin that glowed when she perspired. Her beautiful white teeth were distinguished by a precise upper gap that made her smiles adorable.

Gifty was a very competitive girl who got mad whenever my exam grades were better than hers, especially if we had studied together. I was class captain, and she hated my fair-minded, serious exercise of power. I did not cut her any slack, at least not if others would be punished for the same offense. Gifty loved to chitchat in class, which got her into trouble. But she abhorred the punishment, which usually involved sweeping a classroom or some other part of campus. It wasn't the sweeping itself that annoyed her; it was having to do it at the end of the school day, when other students were heading home with their friends. She possessed what in modern parlance would be described as FOMO, fear of missing out.

One day Gifty had had enough of me constantly writing her up for noisemaking in class, so she enlisted the help of two girls to fight me: Deborah, her coconspirator, and Matilda Walker. When I showed up where they were waiting for me, Matilda was surprised to see that I was the culprit whom she was supposed to fight. Gifty did not know that Matilda was like a sister to me. Her father, Mr. Walker, had been one of my father's best friends. Sometimes I passed by their house on my way to school to receive lunch money. Mrs. Walker called my mother "Ngor," big sister in Kissi. Luckily for me, Matilda told Gifty and Deborah that I was not a bad person. We reconciled and walked home together. When Gifty moved to Nzerekore, Guinea, with her family, Deborah and I remained friends. We were in the same tenth-grade section at Kangoh High School. Gifty visited Gueckedou a couple of times after she moved to Nzerekore, but her family eventually returned to Ghana. She wrote me a letter before she left Nzerekore, and I carried it with me until I moved to Freetown.

CHAPTER 10

A good life does not erupt like a volcano. It unfolds like the petals of a morning flower.

When my mother started to earn some income from her job with IRC, she began to consider moving out of the compound in Bambo. At the beginning of 1998, she rented a two-room flat between Bambo and Mangala. She transformed the living room and piazza into a tailor shop, where she sewed when she was not at the institute. On school days, Musa and Elizabeth walked to Moiwo's house, then continued to my new place, and we walked to school together. Musa and Moiwo were in the twelfth grade, I was a grade below them, and Elizabeth was a grade below me. Elizabeth was a very beautiful girl, so her presence raised our social standing among those who wanted to be her boyfriend, which was almost every boy at Kangoh High School. Some teachers pursued her too, which often created an awkward situation for us. In those days, even though IRC prohibited it, romantic relationships between high school students and their teachers were common in refugee schools.

Teachers dating students was unusual among those who were from the Sierra Leonean school system, where such a practice was severely reprimanded. But it was accepted or at least disregarded by Liberians. It must be noted that although the practice is unethical for other reasons, many Liberian high school students were adults in their twenties or occasionally their thirties. Institutional, fiduciary, conflict-of-interest, and moral rules made such relationships impermissible, but they mostly involved consenting adults. The exchange of sexual favors and of money for grades was also widespread, even though IRC condemned such practices and fired anyone found guilty. It was difficult to police these inappropriate and repulsive practices by a few unscrupulous teachers.

One particular teacher openly used his position for self-enrichment. After every exam, he invited students to his house to see their tentative grades, and if they were dissatisfied, they could obtain a grade hike, for a fee. Those who were going to fail could purchase a passing grade or exchange a certain quantity of their food rations for higher marks. When he needed help with a menial job at home, he requested student volunteers in exchange for bonus grades. This teacher considered my mother a sister, because they were born in the same town and grew up knowing each other, so he never solicited a bribe from me. In any case, the opportunity was not available because I always received high marks in his classes. But it was appalling to watch him turn his profession into a shameless commercial activity. The man was a charlatan, lacking the slightest scruple, and shameless. He even kept track of the names of students who did poorly and reminded them that the deadline was approaching for him to submit grades to the principal's office.

Before we left the Bambo compound, Hawa, my older sister, completed high school and obtained an IRC scholarship to study computer and secretarial science in Conakry. My mother's new job made her busier, so over time she taught me and my brother how to cook. We are both fast learners, and we soon enough acquired decent cooking skills, especially when it came to peanut butter soup, cassava, and potato leaves. My brother and I cooked whenever our mother was unable to do so. When we were children, my mother used to kick us out of the kitchen, jokingly stating that she didn't want the food to smell like testicles. But things had changed, our lives had been disrupted, and she needed help. Those specious gender norms were set aside, and we became our mother's helpers.

We made some shabby meals in the beginning, but as time passed we began to cook spectacular dishes. We knew our mother would eat whatever we made, so it was better when visitors expressed their appreciation for our food. Once, my mother invited a colleague home who exercised no restraint toward the potato-leaf sauce I had made. Afterward, she asked my mother to recommend a maid for her, because whoever had prepared the meal she had just devoured was a fabulous cook. My mother laughed and told her colleague that unless she wanted to take one of her boys, she had no maid. My mother's colleague was visibly impressed. I was proud to receive a neutral party's approval; otherwise, all we had was our mother's appreciation, which is always excellent. Over the years, far away from home, I came to the realization that my mother had taught us those skills because she knew that the time would come when we would be separated from her and would have no sisters or wives to cook our meals. By teaching us essential skills, she would still be taking care of us even when she was absent.

Before the May 1997 coup d'état in Freetown, Sahr Joseph Tolno, my uncle, had sent letters requesting that I move to Freetown and live with his family. Sahr J, as I like to call him, is a man with a pure heart and a good spirit. He takes credit for arranging the relationship between my mother and father. My mother had been sent to Liberia with the idea of betrothing her to her own uncle. When Sahr J heard about the plan, he made an immediate trip to Monrovia to extract his sister. His actions aggravated many family members, but it was a move he remains proud of. He never misses a chance to recount this valorous tale, especially after a few beers. He owned a nightclub in Pendembu, where he met my father, a young man renowned for his wits. My uncle loves to mention how broke my father was, but, as he always emphasizes, he knew that when it came to intellect and respectability, there was no better man in Sierra Leone than my father. My father never attended secondary school. He had gone straight to a Teachers College after standard six and subsequently attended Fourah Bay College. The Catholic Mission later sent him to England for further studies, with the intention of putting him in charge of a local vocational institute.

I sometimes watch my uncle's face when he is telling these stories to my friends. His youthfulness returns, and I can feel the happiness exuded by his laughter. My uncle was at the social prime of his life when he met my father. He was an entrepreneur, with access to unlimited beer (which he loves), lots of female friends, and good music. A recollection of those days of his youth seems to transport my uncle back to the actual experiences. He and my father would have bonded over music. Many years later, my uncle granted me access to his music collection, which almost made me cry, because it looked like a replica of my father's: full of reggae, country music, and pop. There were Eric Donaldson, Eric Clapton, Don Williams, Madonna, Judy Butcher, Phil Collins, Bob Marley, Michael Jackson, Tina Turner, and Dolly Parton. There were also recordings by old-school French folksingers from his time as a student in Strasbourg. But even with their similarity in musical taste, I could never visualize the excitement of the two of them hanging out. My uncle is ebullient, with a manifest joie de vivre, and my father was professorial, even in his most exuberant state. But somehow the vivacious discothèque proprietor and the awkward teacher found a connection so solid that my uncle gave his beloved sister to my father. When my father expressed interest in my mother, my uncle, who was now her guardian, said marriage or nothing. This is how my father, the notorious eligible bachelor of Pendembu at the time, got married.

My uncle never got over the news of my father's sudden death, which left his sister with four children to raise, and he wanted to assist my mother. When my uncle remembers that he never saw my father again after they both left Pendembu, one can almost see the sadness slide down his face like a drop of water on a windshield. He never talks about those feelings, the anger and sense of nothingness left by a civil war that took almost all our joy and robbed us of our dear ones. Those of us who survived cannot remember the good old days without confronting the torment of the tragedy that comes after. When we cannot balance our survival on a pendulum that is constantly swinging between joy and sorrow, good mood and bad mood, we simply do not look back, but go forward like those whose very lives began the day they became survivors. Some of us gain rebirth as survivors; others languish on the sorrowful side of the pendulum, where the torture continues long after the war. To my uncle, I would become a reminder of the man he lost to the war, his beloved brother-in-law, my father.

We finally accepted my uncle's invitation for me to go live with him, and I left Gueckedou without any fanfare. I regretted leaving my mother behind, but we knew that my educational future was better in Freetown. My mother had been preparing me for life away from her. My uncle is a kind man, but my whole family held doubts about his wife, Mrs. Adeyemi Tolno (my Auntie Ade). She had a bad reputation in the family, and my mother wanted me to be equipped to take care of myself if things ever went sour, which is why it took her so long to accept my uncle's offer.

During the 1997 coup d'état, my uncle and his family escaped temporarily to Conakry. They spent more than six months with Mama Yawa, and relatives who visited them there left with a negative impression about their Sierra Leonean in-law. My mother was not worried, because many years before, during a visit to Freetown, she warned Auntie Ade about the possibility that she might someday be taking care of her nephews. "If anything ever happens to my children in your care," my mother warned, "I will come here and beat the heck out of you." Previous encounters between the two held enough proof that my mother never issues vain threats.

The public bus between Gueckedou and Conakry departed on Wednesdays. My mother, Francis, Musa, and a few other close friends came to the station to see me off. I detest good-byes to an emotional core, so when it was time to leave I gave my mother a quick hug and jumped on the bus. It takes too long for me to get over my mother's sadness. I always want my mental picture of her, when I am away, to be one in which she is happy. She gave me the same advice over and over: "Listen to your uncle. He is your father now." She said nothing about doing well in school, because that bit was clear and didn't need to be said. If there was one reason I was leaving my mother to live with an uncle, it was to receive better education, something the refugee camp could not offer.

My Lord dropped by the bus station to wish me luck. Despite his uncontested wisdom, he was not one to give pep talks. He assured me that I would do well wherever I went, and that was enough. He walked away, slowly, as he always did, as if he were alone in the universe and nothing mattered. My uncle later showed me a letter My Lord had written ahead of my trip, stating, "Joseph is a boy you'll really come to love because of his manners and academic output. He is docile, cooperative, and tolerant. For the academic output, you will surely be impressed."

The bus departed for its overnight journey at three p.m. We went through Kissidougou, Faranah, Mamou, and Kindia, arriving in Conakry by eight a.m. I had done this trip a couple of times before, to visit Mama Yawa for holidays. I enjoyed watching the Guinean landscape change as we traveled through all four regions of the country: Guinée Forestière, Haute Guinée, Moyenne Guinée, and Guinée Maritime. When I reached Conakry, I was picked up at the bus station in Madina by my cousin Sia, whom we refer to as Sia Concasseur, to distinguish her from the innumerable Sias in the family. Sia Concasseur is Sahr J's first daughter and was born to a Guinean mother. Concasseur is the name of her Conakry neighborhood. Sia dropped me off at Mama Yawa's place in Hamdallaye. Mama Yawa had been ready for the trip to Freetown and was only awaiting my arrival. George Sandouno, one of my mother's young cousins who had also lived with Sahr J to attend SLGS, led the trip. George is one of those resourceful individuals who know how to find a solution to whatever problem they face. Even though President Tejan Kabbah had been restored to power, major roads to Freetown were still occupied by rebels and renegade soldiers of the Sierra Leone military. It was a risky journey, but those like George, who knew clever drivers, made it back and forth just fine.

There were reports of vehicles being attacked, goods looted, and passengers massacred on the roads between Guinea and Sierra Leone. But when danger becomes the status quo, human beings become accustomed to living dangerously. The war had interrupted local economic activities, and Conakry was the closest source of food. We left Conakry early in the morning in order to reach Freetown before dark. The drive from Conakry to Pamlap, the border town between Guinea and Sierra Leone, was uneventful. We encountered a few internal checkpoints, created by the gendarmes to collect money from Sierra Leoneans and other foreign travelers. There were three checkpoints within a few meters of each other in Pamlap town, where one was expected to pay the *commissaires*, *policiers*, and *gendarmes*. Sometimes random officers also walked around the border town, demanding money from nervous travelers.

We navigated the border posts easier than other passengers because George, who traveled the road frequently, had befriended many of the officers in the three departments. They referred to him as "*mon ami*" and were glad to see him. While his friendship with the officers did not grant us an exemption, it certainly earned us fee reductions and waivers. There were those he promised to "see" on his return trip. He never lied to the officers, and they trusted him. Sometimes there simply wasn't enough cash to tip them all.

Once we paid our dues at the checkpoints, we were allowed to enter Sierra Leonean territory, which was on the other side of the barriers. George knew the reliable drivers, those who could successfully take us through rebel territories in northern Sierra Leone without getting us killed. We boarded a Peugeot 505 with a driver who appeared confident in his ability to get us to Freetown. He knew the major checkpoints and bypasses on the way. In addition to our tickets, the driver collected the money that was required from each passenger at major checkpoints along the way. He was familiar with secret routes around certain rebel territories, but he could not elude all the stops. He also warned us to use the bathroom before boarding because he had no plans to take a break until the next major stop. Driving high speed without stopping was one way to evade rebel ambushes. Vehicles that slowed down on the highway were often attacked and looted, and passengers were sometimes killed or kidnapped. It was a dangerous journey, but the war had gone on for so long that we had grown unwilling to let the rebels control all aspects of our lives.

After more than seven years of war, the country was a carcass of its old self. The rebels had deliberately destroyed roads in order to make them impassable for government military vehicles. Fortunately, we were traveling during the dry season, so all we had to contend with were the deep trenches left by the rains and the dust blown by vehicles traveling at high speed. We galloped through the day, the exposed crevices of our bodies filling with the brown mortar created by a mixture of sweat and dust, and made our way to Freetown. Sometimes we were ordered out of our vehicle for a body search; at other times we stayed in the vehicle while the driver fulfilled the financial obligation of traveling through a country divided between rebels and loyal government soldiers.

After the 1997 coup, the AFRC regime invited RUF rebels to Freetown and made their leader, Foday Sankoh, who was detained in Nigeria on weapons charges, deputy chairman. The two forces united under what was referred to as the "People's Army." This alliance exposed a previously suspected collusion between the rebels and the military described as SOBEL: soldier by day, rebel by night. It was a criminal conspiracy through which members of the military colluded with the rebels they were supposed to be fighting, against the civilians they had taken an oath to protect. When they finally made their alliance official under the banner of a People's Army, our national defense responsibilities fell to ECOMOG, the West African peacekeeping force that would overthrow them and restore President Kabbah to power.

The checkpoint at Mile 91, a town whose name indicates its distance from Freetown, was the most thorough. Like Pamlap, it housed three defense facilities for ECOMOG forces, loyal members of the military, and the Sierra Leone police. All vehicles from Guinea, Liberia, and other parts of Sierra Leone had to get in line to be searched and to produce their customs declaration—whatever the latter was worth in a country at war and with little internal administration. Every passenger had to present a travel document and pay an arbitrary fee, based purely on individual bargaining skill. The vehicles were unloaded and searched. Those importing commodities were required to pay exorbitant fees, sometimes exceeding the price of whatever goods they were bringing. When the searches and transfer of money were completed, a process that took hours, we reboarded our vehicle and continued toward Freetown. Our last checkpoint was Waterloo, a small town not too far from our destination. As soon as we stopped, street vendors, trying to sell all sorts of merchandise, surrounded the vehicle. Portable Tiger generators, producing dull lights and burning fumes, hummed around us. The generators, locally known as Kabbah Tigers, were named in mockery of a president whose failure to provide consistent electricity to Freetown had given rise to the importation of private generators. I thought the derision was unfair, since President Kabbah had only been in power for a year when he was overthrown. When the driver paid the police officers, the wooden barriers were taken down, and we were let through.

It was after midnight when we passed Waterloo. The driver tilted his head toward the passengers in the back and said, "Alhamdulillah! No more checkpoints." It was great news, but because we entered Freetown after midnight, we could not disembark until five a.m., when Muslims wake up for their morning prayers (a measure to prevent rebels from infiltrating the city overnight and to protect passengers from downtown criminals), so we drove through Hastings and headed to Eastern Police Station, where we parked for the night. The police officers searched the vehicle haphazardly and gave us permission to sleep on the long benches in the main hall of the station. I lay on a bench and my aunt covered me with one of her wrappers to protect me from mosquito bites. George spent the night chatting with the officers. I had only begun to sleep when the Muslim call to prayer commenced in the distance. It was morning.

The police officers offered us some water to wash our faces. It took another hour after the call to prayer before merchants began to fill the streets, bikers honked their horns, and drivers warmed the engines of their vehicles, getting ready for a day's work. George chartered a taxi to take us to my uncle's place. He gave the driver some money and told him the address: 7 Andrew Street, Murray Town. We drove through Abacha Street toward Wilberforce Street, crossed Siaka Stevens Street, and turned onto Lightfoot Boston Street. We drove down Kroo Bay quickly, inhaling the pungent stench of morning filth, merged onto Krootown Road, and went down Ascension Town Road. After driving through Congotown, we emerged onto Main Motor Road, Congo Cross. A short drive on Main Motor Road led to a slight right turn onto Murray Town Road.

It dawned on me that I wouldn't be returning to Guinea for a while, and I was about to meet an uncle I did not remember. I was to live with him for as long as it took to complete secondary school and enter college. Better yet, he would become my father. I was extremely nervous, but I kept an open mind. While I was still thinking about my future with an uncle I did not know and what my life was going to become away from my mother, I saw a sign that read "Andrew Street." The driver took a left turn and stopped in front of number seven, my new home.

CHAPTER 11

There will come a time when a principle one
is so certain about becomes questionable.
That is the moment of learning.

The neighborhood was still asleep when we arrived at number seven Andrew Street. I knocked at the door, and my uncle emerged, topless, barefoot, and still trying to get his belt around his waist. He is short and well built. I needed no confirmation of his identity, because his face carries all the marks of my mother's relatives. My uncle and his sisters look identical. Mama Yawa was happy to see her brother. My uncle's laughter and his apparent clumsiness put me at ease. He did not appear to be a rigid man who took himself too seriously. Hawa, my older sister, had assured me of his generosity. When he fled to Conakry as a refugee in 1997, Hawa had been a struggling student there. My uncle, even with his limited resources, visited my sister regularly and took her food supplies. If he was genetically endowed with even half of my mother's and Mama Yawa's kindness, I was certain we would get along.

While we were still greeting each other at the door, my cousin Mariata, Mama Yawa's older daughter, who had lived with my uncle since she was a child, came sprinting out of the house. She was followed by my little cousin Valery, my uncle's three-year-old daughter with Auntie Ade. I was secretly combing the back room with my eyes, looking for Auntie Ade, but she was deliberately taking her time. A few minutes later, she emerged, disinterestedly. She greeted Mama Yawa nonchalantly and nodded her head in my direction. "Good Morning, Auntie," I said, looking at her, but she continued on her way with no real interest in my greetings. My elders say, "Sinister is one who does not return a greeting." It was our first encounter, but first impressions are solid indicators of character. My aunt demonstrated to me, on that first meeting, what many family members had said about her. She lacks traditional manners.

We had traveled across the border and through dangerous rebel territories to get to Freetown, but Auntie Ade made no time to even engage in small talk about our trip. A traditional upbringing requires one to stop everything else to welcome a visitor. An individual could get out of any prior obligation by simply claiming he or she had a guest. But Auntie Ade was different; it did not matter to her that we were there. She went about her morning routine as if her sister-in-law, who had taken care of her in Guinea, and her nephew had not just arrived. My uncle, on the other hand, was excited to see me. It appeared that he had been awaiting my arrival since he returned to Freetown after his brief stay in Guinea as a refugee. He grabbed my little suitcase and told me to follow him. We walked up some wooden stairs to the second floor of the building, where there were an empty parlor and two rooms. My uncle walked into the unfurnished room on the right and put down my suitcase.

"This is your room," he said. "You'll have enough time to clean it later."

"Okay, sir," I responded with genuine appreciation.

I was quietly glad to finally meet my mother's only brother. I had heard about him for years, but I had never really been able to visualize him. He had been a legend of my childhood whose unlimited antics, as told by other members of my family, had made me dream of meeting him. There I was after all these years, not as his visitor or nephew, but as his son.

When we came back downstairs, I was properly introduced to my cousin Mariata. My uncle had visited Mama Yawa some years ago, and Mariata, just a toddler then, had asked to follow him to Freetown. My uncle accepted her request and took her with him.

When I moved to Freetown, Mariata was in junior secondary school (JSS) III, the last year of junior high in Sierra Leone. Mariata was visibly excited to have me around. I was glad to meet her, too.

In spite of her bad attitude, Auntie Ade told her helper, Fatu, to make some breakfast for us. Fatu, who was in her mid-twenties, occupied the second room upstairs and helped Auntie Ade with her chores. She was an unpaid helper who lived as a member of the family. She usually did all the housework, including cooking during weekdays, while Auntie Ade sat there, running her mouth about everyone and everything.

At seven a.m., Auntie Ade walked to Murray Town Municipal Primary School, where she taught. Valery was driven to her nursery school in my uncle's Datsun 120Y. Even though Valery's nursery school was in the same direction as St. Joseph's Secondary School, where Mariata was a student, my aunt prohibited the driver from driving her to school, for no other reason than to make Mariata's life difficult. Every day, my uncle gave Mariata 1,500 leones: 1,000 for her commute and 500 for lunch.

When they had all departed, I sat down with my uncle and Mama Yawa for breakfast. My uncle wasted no time before discussing my schooling. He had received raving reports about my academic performance as a student in Guinea, but he was not quite convinced of the adequacy of the education provided by the refugee schools, especially because he had set his mind on no other school for me than the Sierra Leone Grammar School (SLGS).

I went upstairs and returned with a folder containing my academic records and the recommendations written by my teachers, including My Lord. My uncle looked through the papers, but instead of praising me, he said, "These are very good, but the Sierra Leone Grammar School is an excellent school and I am not sure whether you would be accepted with these refugee papers."

I said nothing. Mama Yawa was visibly offended, but we both held our peace and listened to what he had to say. My uncle was unstoppable in extolling the high academic standards of SLGS, and he wondered aloud whether I might fail to meet the expectations of the principal, A. J. Lasite. My uncle was amazed that Mr. Lasite had even considered the idea of interviewing me for a place at the school. I met the age requirement for senior secondary school (SSS) I, which is the first grade of high school, but I had not taken the Basic Education Certificate Examination (BECE), which had recently become the qualifying entrance exam for secondary school. My uncle was giving me information I couldn't do anything about, and, whether consciously or unconsciously, he was belittling my achievements. I had conquered many odds of survival and presented my uncle with the academic results of my pursuits, but right there, with bread and tea, he reduced all of it to the mere reward of the inflated standards of a refugee school system. Perhaps he was right, but I did not see it that way. I was not so special as to be a recipient of academic rewards from all my teachers.

When he had rambled to his satisfaction, he turned to Mama Yawa and said, "Well, his father was a very intelligent man. If he has even half his father's brain, he will do just fine."

Mama Yawa had had enough. I'd had my fill too, but my mother had taught me not to argue with adults, so I remained silent. When the room was quiet and all we could hear were the distant shouts of waking neighbors and the loud advertisements of hawkers screaming, "Ar get di bread, soap, pepper, gari," Mama Yawa spoke for the first time.

"En tous cas, j'ai entendu que les enfants de Tewa sont très intelligents"—in any case, I have heard that Tewa's children are very intelligent—she said in her soft voice. I knew my aunt was telling her brother to shut up and give me a chance. Mama Yawa's method of chastising people who held wrong views was to offer the truth about their misperception.

My uncle was nervous. He did not want to make a fool of himself in front of Mr. Lasite, undoubtedly the most reputable man in Freetown. My uncle was sure that he could get me into any school in Freetown, even if I showed up with no report card (he still jokes about the fact that he could have enrolled me in one of the most terrible schools in Freetown), but he wanted me to attend SLGS because Mr. Lasite was the only man he had met in Sierra Leone who believed in merit and could not be persuaded by any other means.

"Regentonians are very respected in this country," he said with a prideful smile. SLGS students and graduates are officially known as Regentonians. "If I'd had the opportunity you have now, I would have never gone to any other school, and that's why I want to give every child in my care this opportunity."

My uncle had ensured that many of his nephews and young cousins who stayed with him attended SLGS. George, who had lived with my uncle, was a current student there. My cousin Pascal, my uncle's only son, had passed BECE and was to continue at SLGS. Those who did not receive admission to SLGS had attended St. Edwards or Prince of Wales, the two other schools my uncle respected.

Mariata returned from school and went upstairs, where I sat quietly as my uncle continued to express to my weary aunt his doubts about the chances of my acceptance to SLGS. It came down to the fact that he thought I was timid, unexpressive, and nonchalant. I had not shown any overt excitement about being in Freetown. What my uncle did not know was that I am an introvert, as was my father, the man he had made his sister marry. I try, but it takes me a while to open up to strangers. Even though he is my uncle, I was meeting him properly for the first time. I was a toddler when he left Pendembu. Mariata looked through my academic records and was impressed. "I think Lasite will definitely take you," she said without a shred of doubt. She went on to tell me about the nimbus of prestige surrounding Regentonians and how many boys dream of attending the school. There was one more advantage: the school was only a stone's throw away from Andrew Street.

I went outside, where Mama Yawa was sitting under an apple tree, her lips tightly sealed, the way they always are when she is mad about something. I sat beside her and said nothing. We were both distressed, and Mama Yawa was afraid that from the kind of welcome we had received, Freetown might not have been the best choice for me, and a good-bye might be in the near future. My aunt had always been proud of my academic achievements, but now her brother was questioning their validity and my ability. I felt like an athlete whose title is snatched away based on false accusations of doping. In my case, my uncle implied that I was a mere beneficiary of an inflated grading system, giving no credit to my efforts. His perception of refugee schools in Guinea was that they were utterly substandard. But the IRC had established a very sophisticated refugee school system and employed highly competent instructors like My Lord. Yes, it was a refugee school system, but we did our best to overcome the many limitations of our situation.

Mama Yawa saw that I was upset. I could see from the corner of my eye that she was looking at me. It was a look I had seen many times in my mother's eyes when I was caught in an impossible circumstance and she pitied me. Mama Yawa was furious, but my uncle is her older brother, and she was obliged to listen and wait for the result of our visit to SLGS. When I lifted my head and caught her looking at me, she said in Kissi, "My son, whoever this man is, I hope he sees what your uncle is not seeing, that you are a very smart kid. But if this doesn't work out, we will go back to Guinea, where we were doing just fine."

The verbal assurance that I did not have to stay in Freetown if I didn't want to lightened my mood. I needed the guarantee that I was not condemned to live with my uncle. I had a choice, and that made all the difference.

That evening, we walked around the Murray Town neighborhood. Mariata introduced us to neighbors and friends. Mama Yawa insisted on seeing my cousin Pascal, who had moved out of my uncle's house a long time before. Pascal had not gotten along with his stepmother and had left home to live with friends at Manley Hall on Murray Town Road. His half sister, Sia Tolno, had done the same a few years earlier. My mother and Mama Yawa hated that their brother allowed his new wife to push his children out of his home. It is why Mama Yawa insisted on seeing Pascal. She wanted to be absolutely sure that he was well.

This was my first time to meet Pascal. He bears a stark resemblance to my uncle, except for his rather small eyes. Mama Yawa had not seen him since he was a toddler. During the AFRC coup d'état, my uncle and his wife's family had driven right by Manley Hall and escaped to Guinea, leaving Pascal behind. Sia had found a way to escape to Guinea, but Pascal had had no means, so he stayed in Freetown, enduring the full terror of the AFRC regime.

"What kind of man leaves his children in war?" my mother asked whenever my uncle's action came up in a conversation. "Sometimes I wonder what has gone wrong with my brother."

I learned that if I got into SLGS, Pascal and I would be in the same grade and section. High school education in Sierra Leone is divided into three domains we call "streams": arts, sciences, and commercial. Those interested in the humanities and social sciences enroll in the arts stream. The possibility of being in the same section with Pascal gave me solace. Pascal had been a Regentonian since JSS-I, and so he knew all the other members of his grade. He too was certain that Mr. Lasite would accept me. Although my uncle still had his doubts, my cousins were confident that SLGS would welcome me.

My first impression of Pascal was that he had his share of the sense of humor that runs in our family. I had heard many stories about the maltreatment he'd borne at the hands of his stepmother, but Pascal seemed content. He held no animosity against his father and returned to Andrew Street regularly to visit Mariata. My uncle's response to family rebukes concerning the fact that his children had been expelled from his house was that he'd never kicked them out. He ran a hotel business, Urika River Creek, with French partners in a village called Conakry Dee, so he was often out of town. As a result, he was sincerely oblivious to the abuses his wife dealt to the children under his roof.

When I went to bed that night, my uncle's skeptical voice rang over and over in my head. I thought of the idea that my refugee school grades might have been inflated, and I began to doubt myself. I had willingly left my mother in Guinea to live with my uncle because she believed it was better for my future, but maybe she had placed too much faith in me. I wondered whether all the double promotions I had received in school could have been undeserved accolades. While I lay there worrying that I might soon become a bundle of disappointment to my uncle, it occurred to me that he wasn't really concerned about me, per se; he was nervous about embarrassing himself in front of Mr. Lasite, a man he respected. My uncle may have been impressed with my academic record, but he had set his mind on SLGS because it was the best secondary school in the country, and he was worried about whether my record would be enough to convince Mr. Lasite to accept a student who had not taken the BECE. When this all became clear to me, I slept.

CHAPTER 12

Sometimes it is far better to leave the talking to others.

There are times when one wishes that the night would last forever, when waking up means confronting a dreadful morning. Sometimes, regardless of whether the outcome turns out to be good or bad, life is better with the knowledge of where one stands on the scale of outcomes. The anxiety of visiting SLGS and putting my uncle at ease, or not, shortened my night. I hate stressing about things that I cannot at the moment change. Others might enjoy constant speculation about future events; I would rather wait and deal with the matter itself, no matter how troublesome. One should not weep over the result of an event that has not yet occurred. Instead of spending my energy worrying about the possibility of failure, which is what most people do, I devote my mind to preparing for success. If after my preparation I fail, I prepare again for another attempt or an alternative way forward.

My uncle, Mama Yawa, and I had breakfast together again. My uncle was already dressed and ready for the trip to SLGS. He repeatedly reviewed my papers and kept making the same skeptical comments about my eligibility. After breakfast, I went upstairs and put on my best clothes. I knew that my uncle would find an issue with whatever I wore that morning. I had already profiled him and mentally catalogued his ticking points. I wore black pants, a white shirt with short sleeves, and black boots. I looked like a well-dressed cowboy. My uncle said I needed dress shoes and complained that my belt buckle was too big. He offered a pair of his shoes and a simple belt, which I refused. He got upset and started to talk endlessly about how important it was to dress to impress. Mama Yawa replied that I looked great and he should just take me like I was.

My uncle understood that I was determined not to change anything I was wearing. If Mr. Lasite was going to reject me based on my boots and a decent belt buckle, then I wouldn't sulk over failing to become a member of his institution. In any event, I was not yet his pupil, so it was still my right to wear whatever I preferred. I was defiant. It is what happens when I feel that a criticism is not constructive.

When my uncle got over my dress code, he and I began our walk up the hill toward SLGS. The school stands at the peak of Macaulay Street, which is adjacent to Andrew Street. We took a shortcut between two houses. Neighbors popped their heads out of their windows to catch a glimpse of the stranger in their neighborhood. I was cognizant of their subtle presence, which I pretended not to notice.

I learned that day that my uncle does not do well in high temperatures. During our climb up the hill he began to sweat profusely, and by the time we were halfway his shirt was drenched in sweat. We walked past the cotton tree at the edge of the SLGS compound and entered through the main gate. School was not yet in session, so the campus was empty besides the presence of Mr. Lasite and the bursar. We went up the stairs to the second floor and walked to the west wing of the building, where the principal's office is located. My uncle nervously knocked on the door, and a small man, neatly dressed and simple looking, emerged. His only distinguishing feature was a rather slight goatee.

"Hello, Mr. Joseph!" He knew my uncle well. By the time my uncle returned his greeting, Lasite had moved on.

"I believe this is the young man you told me about! Well, let's see his documents." He took my papers and went into his office while we waited. My uncle was still sweating like a laborer.

A few minutes later, Mr. Lasite invited us into his office. He offered me a chair in front of his desk. My uncle sat to my left. Mr. Lasite went through my papers once more before turning to address me. My uncle's eyes were wide open.

"So, young man," he said, "what profession are you interested in?"

"Journalism," I responded without wasting time. A delay would have allowed my uncle to volunteer an answer.

"Fantastic! That is great!" Mr. Lasite reacted with genuine excitement.

While I was reveling in his approval, secretly smiling about how smoothly the meeting had gone so far, he turned to my uncle and said, "Mr. Joseph, your nephew seems like an excellent pupil, and there is room for him at the Sierra Leone Grammar School."

"Thank you very much, sir!" my uncle replied with a huge smile on his face. He wanted to chat, but Mr. Lasite is not a small-talker. He congratulated me with a handshake and welcomed me to SLGS. He told my uncle to collect my textbook list at the bursar's office and gave us a letter to deliver to the office of the West African Examination Council (WAEC) for me to be added to their database.

My uncle was happy, but he was not the type to dwell on success. He thought I was lucky, and since he no longer had to worry about my getting into SLGS, his new enterprise was to impress on me that I had a duty to *succeed* at SLGS, as if I had come all the way to Freetown to frolic. He would not stop talking about the fact that Mr. Lasite does not tolerate repeaters.

"If you fail, he will kick you out," he said, over and over. I said nothing throughout his rant. Sometimes it is better to let people do their pointless talking.

Mama Yawa was sitting under the apple tree again, looking in the direction we had taken, nervously awaiting our return. As we approached, she ignored my uncle and looked straight at me. I let my uncle do the talking, but I conveyed the outcome of our trip with a wide smile. Mama Yawa received my message and smirked in return.

"Your nephew has been accepted!" my uncle said. "But you'd better tell him to study hard, because that school is a no-nonsense school."

Mama Yawa wasn't buying any more of his negativity and doubt. "This kid has been doing well all his life. I'm sure he won't stop now," she retorted.

My uncle was happy too. He had expected a crisis, but none had occurred. Mr. Lasite had not questioned the authenticity of my documents or even suggested that my grades were inflated because they'd been earned from a refugee school system. One of Mr. Lasite's greatest qualities as a principal is his ability to look at a pupil and determine his level of motivation. He knew from our first meeting that I am motivated to learn. My recommendation letters may have told him so, and he was willing to give me the benefit of whatever doubt he may have had. Pupils are rarely accepted to SLGS without the required grade from a national entrance exam, but Mr. Lasite knew that behind those low-quality printed papers bearing faded IRC logos was a young man determined to *pursue* knowledge—a Regentonian, or "Oxford," as my classmates eventually nicknamed me. Many years later, when I returned to campus to obtain my transcript and a recommendation, Mr. Lasite knew exactly what to write: "An all-rounder of high academic ability."

My uncle grabbed his keys and opened a storage room filled with books he had stored before escaping to Guinea. "There, some of those books belonged to your father. They are yours now."

I spent the rest of the afternoon cleaning the books and rearranging them in my room. There were volumes on every subject matter, including many of the early publications of the Heinemann African Writers Series and the Bhagavad Gita. I did not know which of the books specifically had belonged to my father, but that did not prevent me from imagining the days when he sat quietly with one of them and transcended the world around him. I flipped through the pages, looking for any evidence of my father, but there was none. My father did not write in the margins of books. When Mama Yawa saw the number of books I had inherited, she made a joke to the effect that perhaps it was unnecessary for me to enroll in school when I could just stay home and read them.

Maya Yawa stayed for a few more days after my acceptance to SLGS. Before returning to Conakry she told me that if my living situation did not work out, I should simply call her. She also reminded me to take care of Mariata. I was excited about school, but I would not start until January of the following year. I had nothing to do till then, so I read and reread. I even read the Gita without knowing what I was reading. Like most Sierra Leoneans, my religious knowledge was limited to Christianity and Islam. It was when I read Gandhi's autobiography in college that I realized the importance of the Gita. It was so fascinatingly dense that I do not recall any of it. I was enthralled by the language and images, but trying to hold any of it in my memory felt like pouring water into a flour sifter.

My uncle also gave me some music cassettes. My favorites were Prince Nico Nbarga, Sonny Okosun, and Fela Anikulapo Kuti. I loved Okonsun's track "African Soldier," in which he salutes black revolutionaries such as Shaka Zulu, Patrice Lumumba, Nelson Mandela, Julius Nyerere, Desmond Tutu, Steve Biko, Muhammad Ali, Martin Luther King Jr., Marcus Garvey, and the like.

When I was a kid, I used to hear my mother sing Fela's songs, but I never had the opportunity to listen to his lyrics until I moved to Freetown. Fela would become one of the African philosophers and political activists I most admired. Music was his medium of communication. With the exception of Nelson Mandela and Desmond Tutu, I have not yet heard another African who speaks such clear truths to power. I later wrote one of my strongest philosophy research papers on one of his tracks, "Suffering and Smiling," in which he captures some of the hypocrisies appertaining to religious practices in many African societies. Africans continue to pay for the wealth and luxury of religious ministers while they themselves languish in inhuman, inconceivable squalor.

Fela was not singing against religion; he was protesting a blatant deviation from the doctrines of love and compassion that underpin many religions. Our evangelists have abandoned the foundational ideals of the messages they purport to spread. All over Africa, one can see the open collusion between politicians and these apostles to exploit the poor. In "Suffering and Smiling," Fela laments African genuflection to the afflictions sprinkled by priests and politicians. We smile passively as our leaders exploit our resources and violate our rights while we are told to turn the other cheek. The African "man of God" is beyond reproach, and his blessings are delivered at the tabernacle of unchallenged truths. In the heads of our poor captives of religion, there is no blame too irrational for God to bear. It is as they sing in that old African spiritual: "Cast your burden unto Jesus." Who else is strong enough to bear the misfortunes of the world?

When we enter a bus or other public transportation and there are forty-nine sitting and ninety-nine standing, "Nah God." When we pay our electricity and water bills, but there is no electricity or water supply, "Nah God." When taxes are levied but no schools are built, no roads are constructed, no hospitals are available for the sick, and children die from curable diseases, "All nah God." We cling to God through his earthly apostles and keep ourselves shackled to the metallic rod of suffering, awaiting deliverance. But:

> Woe unto them that call evil good, and good evil; that say darkness for light, and light for darkness; that say bitter for sweet, and sweet for bitter! Woe unto them that are wise in their own eyes, and prudent in their own sight! Woe unto them that are mighty to drink wine, and men of strength to mingle strong drink: Which justify the wicked for reward, and take away the righteousness of

the righteous from him! Therefore as the fire devoureth the stubble, and the flame consumeth the chaff, so their root shall be as rottenness, and their blossom shall go up as dust: because they have cast away the law of the Lord of hosts, and despised the word of the Holy One of Israel. (Isaiah 5:20-24).

I read for three months. I even read many of the volumes on my three-year book list for SLGS. I left the house only for walks. Murray Town is a small community, so news of my arrival spread. Every time I walked around the neighborhood, people randomly called on me to clarify my lineage. Some believed I was my uncle's biological child, but others thought I resembled another member of my family they had met. My mother had visited a few years earlier, and many neighbors remembered her.

"Your mother is such a nice woman," those who knew her said to me. My mother is the sort of person who shows up in a new place, and a short while later one would think she had lived there all her life. She had visited her brother for a brief period a long time before, but many people on Andrew Street still considered her a friend. There were those, of course, who could not be convinced that I was not my uncle's biological son because of my resemblance to him.

My uncle brought home an old mountain bike from Lungi that I rode in the evenings. The bicycle allowed me to meet many Murray Town girls. They wanted me to teach them how to ride my bike, but I often refused because I was too shy to say yes. There was one girl, though, whom I couldn't resist. Her name was Musu. One day Musu and her friends stopped me during my evening ride.

"Let me see your bike," she said.

I got off the bike for her to take a look, but she sat on it instead. Her friends began to giggle, and that is when I realized that they had planned the ambush.

"Now, you have to teach me how to ride," she said, turning her freshly greased face in my direction. She was beautiful, and I was glad she was on my bike. Her butt cheeks, contained by a short hand-me-down cotton skirt, popped out on either side of my tiny bicycle seat like the two sides of a mini calabash. I spent the whole evening pushing her around on my bike. She laughed the entire time and made no serious efforts to ride the bike. I liked Musu. After that, we met every weekend for riding lessons, but I don't think she ever learned how to ride a bike.

I met many boys too. Most of them were Regentonians who would be in my grade. Mariata had bragged to them that her cousin would soon become the top-ranking pupil at the school. One of them, my friend Alex Bindi (A-Boy), was not convinced. A-Boy was a friend of the highest-ranking student at the time, a Regentonian by the name of Carlton Carew. Every Regentonian I met spoke about the genius of Carlton Carew. A-Boy visited regularly to jokingly taunt Mariata that her "village boy" cousin had no chance at SLGS. As soon as I realized that A-Boy was a joker, I smiled at the ongoing debate between him and Mariata concerning my academic future. It would have been futile to defend myself against someone who enjoyed being silly, so I never tried.

As the weeks passed, I began to feel at home in Murray Town. Pascal visited often, and neighbors invited me to events. Sometimes I found a corner and sat there until the end of the event. I left parties before I was dragged to the dance floor. George visited on Sundays, and we rode our bikes to Aberdeen Beach. Most Freetownians only went to the beach on Sundays and other major holidays. George loved the Chez-Nous bar and restaurant, so we always went there to eat and dance. Other times, he bought liters of palm wine, which we drank as we walked up and down the beach. Here, too, George knew many people. He reminded me of my mother. My brother and I used to hate walking home with her, especially when we were hungry, because she stopped every few steps for a conversation with someone she knew.

At the end of November 1998, the residents of Freetown were pre-occupied with Christmas plans, but underneath the shopping and season's greetings lay a surreal silence, the sort that drowns out the loudest noise. Rumors were circulating that AFRC and RUF rebels, who had been driven out by ECOMOG forces less than a year earlier, were advancing toward Freetown. There were those who put their faith in the ECOMOG forces now in charge of national security, but there were others, like me, who feared the worst might happen. I had seen these reactions to rumors of rebel invasions before. It is a conscious denial of what may be true for a temporary respite in the hope that it might not occur. An escape would be too inconvenient if the rumors turned out to be false. The trauma of war begins with rumors of war. Agonizing over whether to flee and leave familiar life behind, or stay put and bet on providence, is depressing. Many people died during the Sierra Leonean and Liberian civil wars because they did not escape town early enough.

We entered December without any rebel attack. ECOMOG continued to assure us that Freetown was safe. Tangays, an annual cultural festival held at the Stevens Stadium, proceeded as usual. Every evening, I rode my bike to the stadium to enjoy the festivities. There were traditional wares from all over the country, cultural dances, religious revivals, and dance clubs. I danced sometimes, but most of the time I just walked around, people-watching. The war was ongoing, but Freetown was alive and free.

Christmas came and went. The new year dawned without trouble. On Christmas Day, Mariata took me to St. George Catholic Church in Murray Town. I spent New Year's Day riding up and down the beach on my bike. It seemed everyone in Freetown was at the beach that day, and there was no apparent sign of danger or fear. Folks were dancing and having a wonderful time. Everywhere I went, crowds of people sang, "Happy New Year, we nor die oh, tell god tenki for we life." Happy New Year, we did not die. Thank God for our lives.

They were glad to be alive in the New Year, but many wouldn't be for long. On January 6, 1999, the rebels invaded Freetown.

CHAPTER 13

When evildoers strike, we should respond with
an abundant measure of love to counteract
their taint on our pursuit of peace.

The Sierra Leonean civil war started with the RUF invasion
in 1991, but a year later the Sierra Leone Army overthrew
President Joseph Momoh and made twenty-five-year-old Valentine
Strasser head of the National Provisional Ruling Council (NPRC)
and head of state. Strasser was president until 1996, when he was
overthrown by a countercoup led by Julius Maada Bio, a member
of his governing Supreme Council of State. Bio transferred power
to President Tejan Kabbah after a democratic election was held in
1996. A year later, AFRC overthrew President Kabbah and invited
RUF to Freetown.

In 1998, ECOMOG invaded Sierra Leone and liberated Freetown. President Kabbah was reinstated, but most of the country
remained under AFRC/RUF control. Elsewhere in the country, various militia groups had emerged: Kamajor, Donso, Kabras, Gbeti,
and Tamaboro. Each of these names translates to *hunter*. When
the people realized that the country's military was colluding with
rebels to torture, rape, and murder them, they assembled in their
traditional society bushes to train and consecrate militiamen to
defend their towns. Traditional hunting societies had always been
part of Sierra Leonean ethnic existence, but when they became
hunters of people rather than beasts, the conflict was transformed
into an Armageddon wrought by competing "immortals" vying for
political power.

RUF invaded Sierra Leone with assistance from NPFL rebels from Liberia, who claimed to be immortal and immune to bullets. Rumors of their supposed immortality spread fear among Sierra Leoneans. When the militia hunters joined the conflict against the rebels and their coconspirators, their only choice in the scheme of things was to express themselves with a level of supernatural terror that could usurp RUF's claim to the underworld. The various factions walked around decked out in human body parts, wigs, vestments dug out of graves, and other juju ornaments. This is how the Sierra Leonean civil war became a conflict among demonic factions competing to out-devil each other.

The militia groups were all male, except for the Tamaboro, which enlisted two notorious female combatants known as Marie Keita and Willimina Fofana. The latter obtained notoriety for her indiscriminate use of rocket-propelled grenades against areas perceived as rebel territories. These women worked with a local marabout known as Dembasso Samura. Keita and Samura were later captured and butchered with machetes because of the belief that their bodies were immune to bullets.

All hunter militia forces were later grouped under one Civil Defense Force (CDF) to assist with ECOMOG counteroffensives against the rebels. CDF was under the command of Chief Sam Hinga Norman, who later became Deputy Defense Minister. While some believe that the Kamajor militia was created from supernatural instructions received in the dreams of three women, it was actually created by Chief Norman and a few other politicians. Chief Norman, who had been a member of the Sierra Leone Army, was a skillful soldier. He was also regent chief of Jaiama Bongor chiefdom when he began to train the first Kamajor militia. The Kamajor assumed its supernatural reputation when a marabout named Alieu Kondewa joined the movement as chief initiator of recruits. The ancestors allegedly chose Kondewa to be their earthly representative.

The hunter groups were founded at a time when the people had no other option to defend themselves. The SOBEL had embarked on the mass conscription of children, rape, chopping off of limbs, and diamond mining. By the time President Kabbah was reinstated by ECOMOG in 1998, most of Sierra Leone had already been destroyed and thousands of people killed. Another large population languished in refugee camps throughout West Africa. CDF and ECOMOG forces were the only groups standing between the people and the rebels, whose intent was to exterminate everyone who objected to their reach for power and diamonds. CDF was an inadequately trained force that relied for prowess on the ancestors and a hazy belief in their own immortality. ECOMOG was a peacekeeping force, which at this juncture was frustrated by the protracted civil war and its incapacity to wipe out the rebels. The rebels, for their part, were invigorated by the leadership of a Sierra Leone Army officer by the name of Solomon A. J. (SAJ) Musa. SAJ Musa was the commander of the AFRC/RUF force that entered Freetown in January 1999.

I went to bed on January 5 looking forward to the start of school the next day. My uncle had paid for my uniform: a white shirt, khaki pants, and a purple and gray striped necktie. I was so excited that I couldn't fall asleep. I lay in bed and reflected on the struggles I had been through, what my life could have been had the war not happened, and whether I would be in Freetown now had my father not died. At 3:30 a.m., after tossing and turning for hours, I reached for the transistor radio I had brought from Guinea, pulled out the antenna, and turned it on. The habit of listening to the radio when I cannot fall asleep I inherited from my father. I tuned to FM 96.6, the local channel for the BBC World Service.

Network Africa, a program of exclusively African news, was just starting its daily broadcast. One of the headlines that morning was a government official calling on Freetown residents to stay indoors because the city was under attack. It seemed like a dream, but I lay awake. There was no need for further assurance from the radio, because the shooting above the city was loud enough. I sat up on the edge of my bed. When I was a Sunday school boy, I wondered what Job, Abraham, and other biblical figures who were tested by God had felt. Did Abraham ever think that instead of what he believed was the voice of God, he might have been losing his mind? Freetown was invaded on the very morning I thought my life was going to take a new turn and my tribulations would be over. If God was testing me, I was no longer in exam mood.

I was on the front line again, only this time with no escape plan. I sat on the edge of my bed for almost an hour, listening to commentaries about the invasion, switching between BBC and RFI, expecting good news. Then the war began in earnest: thundering sounds of heavy artillery, accompanied by the clatter of small machine guns. It was still dark outside, so I could see tracer bullets moving across the sky like shooting stars. As the rhythmic sound of assorted weapons echoed in the distance, ECOMOG Dassault/Dornier Alpha jets whistled through the clouds, dropping heavy explosives around the city. None of it was new, but this time I really thought it might be the end for me. AFRC/RUF rebels had returned to Freetown not only to retake power, but also to exact revenge against civilians who had not supported their regime, which had produced international condemnations and their subsequent removal from power.

When my mind, which had wandered in search of meaning, returned to me, I walked downstairs where my uncle, his wife, and his daughter lay flat on their bedroom floor. Mariata emerged from her room, looking for answers, but I had none. I told her to stay away from the windows, and I sat in the living room with my radio. The exterior walls of the first floor were constructed from a mixture of concrete and red stones. It would have taken an artillery shell to penetrate the walls. My uncle came out of his room and found me sitting in the living room, reading a newspaper.

"Mr. Man, are you not afraid?" he asked.

"Uncle, when death comes, it doesn't matter whether one is sitting in a chair or hiding under a bed," I replied.

We talked for a while about what might happen without mentioning what we were both thinking: *Are we going to die today?*

My aunt stayed in the bedroom with Valery. Mariata was eavesdropping on our conversation. When my uncle returned to his room, she quietly withdrew to hers, and I remained in place, reading and listening to the news.

By sunrise, the firing had died down a little. The government used the BBC to warn civilians to stay indoors. Those of us relatively far from the front line stayed in our houses, but those whose neighborhoods had fallen to the rebels, especially those in the east of Freetown, had no choice. The rebels forced them out of their houses and tortured, raped, and killed them. Those whose lives were spared were placed ahead of advancing rebels as human shields and told to sing, "We want peace, we want peace!" ECOMOG found it difficult to distinguish civilians from fighters, and as a result many people died. It was important not to let the city fall to the rebels again, no matter the consequences of defending it.

News came in that the president had fled the country, but interviews with government officials and ECOMOG commanders refuted it. It was essential to assure the public that their president had not abandoned the country. As long as the president was in town, there was hope that ECOMOG would continue to defend the city.

I heard a commotion outside. I peered through the window curtains and saw a few ECOMOG soldiers in ambush position. Two others were pouncing on two boys, kicking them and hitting them with gun butts. The boys were Ali and Tutu, apprentices at our neighbor's garage. Ali and Tutu were also fare collectors on a minivan that belonged to my uncle. They were "garage boys," but they could have stayed in our neighbor's house or ours. Ali slept on a small bed in my room on many occasions when he came home late from driving my uncle's minivan, which ran between Freetown and Waterloo.

What had possessed those boys to choose the belly of a minivan parked on Andrew Street on that ungodly morning, only they knew. They were shirtless, as always, but this time it mattered. They were both younger than seventeen, half-naked, and camping in a vehicle in a city under attack. Everything about them was indicative of child soldiers—the bane of ECOMOG's countermeasures. Most adults lean instinctively toward protecting children, but when children become angels of death, a peacekeeping force must act against its instinct. A war involving intoxicated children as enemies is not an easy battle for a professional army.

"Are you rebels?" the ECOMOG soldiers asked as they double-kicked and stepped on Ali and Tutu, gun nozzles in firing position.

"Oga, I beg, we nor to rebel." Oga—boss in Nigerian pidgin—we are not rebels. They cried as the soldiers kicked them into a nearby ditch. That was often where they executed captured rebels. The boys realized what was about to happen and screamed louder.

"Oga, everybody know we nah ya! Ask anyone normor." Everybody knows us here. Just ask anyone.

"If people know you, why are you in that van at this time?" one of the soldiers asked.

"We bossman, sir, we bossman tell we say we kin sleep dae." Our boss told us we could sleep there.

"Who your bossman?"

"Mr. Sahr!" My uncle.

"Where is he? Where does he live?"

Ali and Tutu pointed in my direction. I moved away from the window and returned to the couch. The two ECOMOG soldiers were walking toward our door. The others remained in position, watching Ali and Tutu, who were kneeling in the ditch.

The soldiers knocked on our door. My uncle emerged from his room. He was unsure whether to answer or not. I indicated to him that either he opened the door or the soldiers would break it down. He continued toward the door but stopped suddenly and turned toward me.

"Should I put on a shirt?" Again, all I could think of was the fact that it did not matter to a dead man whether he was dressed or not. But I put my sarcasm aside and answered my uncle earnestly.

"Yes, it's probably better."

Auntie Ade heard us and rushed out with a T-shirt, which my uncle proceeded to put on, inside out. He opened the door while I watched from the living room.

"Are you Mr. Sahr?" one of the ECOMOG soldiers asked.

"Yes, I am." My uncle spoke excellent English. He was flaunting his education to save his life.

"Do you know those boys out there, Ali and Tutu?"

"Yes, they are apprentices I help." His answer satisfied the ECO-MOG soldiers that Ali and Tutu were not child soldiers.

"Why is it that you instructed them to stay out there while you are in here with your family?" The ECOMOG soldier was furious.

"I would never do such a thing," my uncle responded. He told the ECOMOG soldiers that he had not seen Ali and Tutu since the previous day. He, too, was surprised that they were out there. The ECOMOG soldiers thanked my uncle and walked away.

Although my uncle's nightmare was over, circumstances were not so kind to Ali and Tutu. The ECOMOG soldiers beat them to a pulp. Tutu had braids, another marker of child soldiers. The soldiers brought out a razor and shaved their heads right there, in the ditch. When they were done, the soldiers kicked Ali and Tutu in the buttocks and told them to disappear into our neighbor's house. Ali and Tutu ran faster than lightning. When the situation was over, the other soldiers emerged from their positions and continued their operation. Ali and Tutu had been lucky. Many other Murray Town boys would not be so fortunate at the hands of ECOMOG soldiers.

The rebels advanced deeper into Freetown, but by nightfall they had not yet reached Murray Town, even though a few of them had already infiltrated the city. They hid in neighborhoods as dormant combatants waiting for their comrades to get through. As darkness returned, the firing became sporadic. Ms. Ina, our neighbor, was afraid of sleeping in her wooden house, the same house Ali and Tutu had run into, so she came over to stay with us. Ms. Ina was the mother of one of Auntie Ade's best friends who had gone to the U.S. some years before. Ms. Ina was like a grandmother to all her neighbors' children, including me. She shared Fatu's room for the night.

We went to bed thinking that things might have gotten better; ECOMOG might have pushed the rebels out. It was later revealed that the rebels were regrouping because their commander, SAJ Musa, had been killed in an explosion when one of his amateur warriors set an ordnance depot on fire. SAJ Musa's death left the rebels with no central command to dictate strategy.

But although the rebels were slowed down by this setback, they were not defeated. Fighting recommenced later that night. Ms. Ina made the poor choice of looking out the window right about the same time that rebels unleashed a fusillade of antiaircraft artillery rockets. The rockets traveled in an arc, and even though their target was in the center of town, far from where we were, the darkness magnified the appearance of the rockets, and it looked like they were coming straight toward the old lady. Ms. Ina dashed out of the room, fell, and rolled down the stairs, screaming hysterically. We convinced her that the rebels were still far from us, but we did not persuade her to go back upstairs. It is often the case that when someone stands vis-à-vis their mortality, imagined or real, their whole being remains shaken for a long time. Incidents similar to the one Ms. Ina experienced left many people severely traumatized for a while. Even for a precocious survivor of many attacks like me, nothing I had witnessed before matched what spread across the Freetown sky that night.

Dark smoke rose into the sky as rebels set houses on fire. Different sizes of flames transported by fast-moving rockets interlaced the sky. ECOMOG Alpha jets seemed to be in permanent action. The rebels were determined to either take over Freetown or destroy it. But ECOMOG refused to submit to a humiliating defeat from a ragtag force in demonic attire. The news on BBC and RFI reminded us of our fate if the rebels were to take control of the whole city. The rebels, who were mainly AFRC youths from the Freetown boroughs, knew their city better than ECOMOG forces, who were mostly Nigerians. Every corner of Freetown became a battlefield as the rebels split into small groups and popped up in different parts of the city, using captured civilians as their shields. A few days later, an ECOMOG commander admitted that forcing the rebels out of Freetown was going to take some time because his soldiers were using a tactic he referred to as FIBA: fighting in built-up areas. He meant fighting in a city without turning it into a total apocalyptic theater.

I spent my days in the living room, watching my uncle, his wife, and his child compete for space wherever they felt safe within the four corners of their bedroom. They did their bodily functions in buckets, but I still used the outdoor latrine. As disgusting as that latrine was, I hated shitting in a bucket more than watching maggots crawl out of our full hole in the ground, with a corroded, crumbling shelter. It was the first experience of life on a war front for everyone except me.

After the city had been under siege for days, ECOMOG began to let people out for short intervals to look for food and water. We had some food in the house, and we consumed it piecemeal. Being full was not important; it only mattered that one had *something* to eat. There were those who had no food after the first few days of lockdown. Neighbors who had plenty of food shared with friends who had none. One of my uncle's cousins, who lived in the east of Freetown, escaped with his two teenage children, Sahr and Kumba, and came to live with us.

After years of evading death, one develops a nonchalant attitude toward war. There was no need for an escape plan, because getting out of Freetown alive was practically impossible. I spent my days listening to explosions and propaganda music from the incumbent government. FM 98.1, or Radio Democracy, was programmed by whichever DJ had been last at the station to repeatedly play songs about democracy that had been produced for the 1996 elections. We couldn't turn off the radio because even though there was hardly any news, we kept hoping a ceasefire would be announced. While civilians were being slaughtered on the streets of Freetown, we listened to songs with such lyrics as "Democracy, democracy, the government of the people, by the people, for the people, naim we want nah Salone." But amid the propaganda songs, an album by Buju Banton, a reggae artist, had somehow made it to the playlist. The song "Single Parent" transported me to Guinea, where I knew my mother was having sleepless nights worrying about me. Sometimes I couldn't help but think that I might never see her again. I tried not to consider what would become of my mother if I died. She would have felt responsible for sending me to Freetown before the war was completely over. But how could she have known?

Death ruled us for weeks. The shootings and bombardments made sleep impossible. During the day, rebels and ECOMOG soldiers killed at will. The rebels killed to affirm their rule of engagement: Operation No Living Thing. They killed those they could not conscript, raped girls and their mothers, and murdered others who were useless to them. ECOMOG sometimes killed indiscriminately because they could not distinguish civilians from rebels. The rebels fought mostly in civilian clothing, so without weapons it was impossible to know who the killers were. This is how innocent civilians lost their lives to ECOMOG bullets. It was not uncommon during the war to hear about civilians who spent weeks escaping rebel-controlled areas, just to get killed at an ECOMOG check-point. ECOMOG stopped taking chances by presuming people to be civilians after too many of their comrades got killed by rebels pretending to be civilians. Hardly any international law was observed during the war in Sierra Leone; we were all at the mercy of each other's brutal instincts.

On days when the curfew was lifted, between three p.m. and five p.m., I quietly left the house and walked around the neighborhood. The streets were desolate, except for the multiple ECOMOG check-points one had to go through. When stopped at a checkpoint, one was expected to provide a reason for being outside. Those suspected of being rebels were killed instantly. I had an old IRC student ID that I showed at checkpoints. They searched us and inspected our bodies to make sure that we had no AFRC/RUF tattoos. The rebels tattooed their conscripted fighters in order to deter them from escaping. It was a strategy to maintain loyalty, because those caught with rebel tattoos were killed. Children who were conscripted and marked could not escape.

One afternoon, during a curfew intermission, I decided to walk to Congo Cross, where Grandma Oju and Grandpa Davis, Auntie Ade's parents, lived. Rumors had reached us that George had been killed, his corpse left in front of a building in Brookfields. The rebels had been pushed out of the center of town, and the curfew intermission was extended to six p.m. When I told Mariata that I was going out to find out about George, Sahr, the boy who had come to live with us, decided to follow me. As it turned out, I should have stopped him.

We encountered no problems on our way to Congo Cross. People hurried about, trying to find food for their families before the curfew ended. Others sought safety wherever it seemed promising. When we got near Grandma Oju's house on Main Motor Road, in Congo Cross, I recognized a man on a bicycle riding toward us. It was George! He was alive and well. We entered the compound and greeted Grandma Oju and Grandpa Davis. They were healthy and in good spirits. I was excited to see that George was safe. I decided that we should return home well before the end of the curfew intermission, because Sahr was with me. Another reason I wanted us to be home early was that his father hadn't yet realized he was out of the house. This is when the folly of allowing him to come with me actually dawned on me.

George sent word to my uncle that he would come to Murray Town as soon as the war was over. He had to get back home now, before the curfew intermission ended.

When Sahr and I started our return journey, a massive crowd, some carrying bundles, others their dying relatives, was heading down Main Motor Road toward Wilkinson Road, the same direction we were heading. Their number increased by the minute. It seemed that they had just been liberated from rebel-controlled areas. Among them were some whose limbs had been recently chopped off by rebels; they badly needed medical attention. I told Sahr to walk faster because I did not want to be part of the crowd; it seemed destined for a bad end. Many of them had no idea where they were going, and it wasn't long before the beginning of curfew.

We hurried but did not get far. By the time we reached Murray Town Juncture, ECOMOG had set up an emergency checkpoint. There was fear that some of the displaced people heading toward the west of Freetown might be rebels. Chaos ensued. ECOMOG soldiers were asking for IDs in a situation in which many people had barely escaped with their lives. Young boys suspected of being rebels were pushed to the side. I saw a young boy being pulled by his pants while he screamed, "Me nor to rebel!" I am not a rebel!

While the turmoil ensued, a military vehicle arrived with Julius Spencer, Minister of Information. He was dressed in full military uniform, even though he was not a soldier. The minister ordered ECOMOG not to let anyone beyond that point. He wanted everyone to return to Stevens Stadium in the center of town. Folks began

ADAMALUI

to push each other in a demonstrative rejection of the order. I told Sahr to follow me. I knew that things were about to get out of hand, and I did not want to be there when that happened. I already knew Murray Town well, and I knew how to get home without using the main road.

We walked toward the coast, to an area known as Banana Water. We successfully wove through houses, walking adjacent to Murray Town Road, and made our way toward the shore. We came upon one obstacle I had not anticipated: the Sierra Leone Navy Headquarters is located on that same stretch of coast, and there is no way around the compound. When we neared the headquarters, we had no choice but to head up to Murray Town Road. We emerged onto Murray Town Road, and it was as if the ECOMOG soldiers had been waiting for us all along.

"Halt!" ordered the ECOMOG soldiers at the navy checkpoint. They were to our right, in the direction we were heading. On the left was the Murray Town Ordnance, where there was another checkpoint. Then up the hill, toward Murray Town Barracks, was another checkpoint. We stood in the middle of the three.

Two ECOMOG officers from the navy checkpoint walked toward us, their guns drawn and ready to fire. I was afraid, but many years of this sort of scenario had taught me that the best way to stay alive was to avoid panic. While the soldiers walked toward us, I told Sahr to stay calm. One of them asked for our names and addresses. He also asked for our IDs. When he was satisfied with the information we provided, he lifted our shirts and inspected our bodies for rebel tattoos.

"Why are you out here? Don't you know there is curfew?" He was not interested in an answer. "Come, follow me," he continued. We walked with him to the checkpoint. He consulted with his friends while we waited. I knew they were not going to kill us, but I wondered what they were going to do to us. Sahr was crying, and he attempted to explain that he was not a child soldier.

177

The ECOMOG soldier returned to us after speaking with his associates. I was eager to hear what he had to say. He said, "Hey, my friends, I am going to count from one to five. By the time I am done, you should have disappeared from this street."

Sahr was listening intently, and I knew what to do. I had never run so fast in my life. Sahr was close behind. Instead of running all the way to Andrew Street, which was far from the Navy Headquarters, we darted off Murray Town Road and up to Somerset Street, which cut through the other streets. We stopped running as soon as we were off Murray Town Road and out of range of the ECOMOG soldiers. Running through the neighborhood would have caused others to either think that we were rebels ourselves, or that we were running away from rebels.

When we got home, I informed my uncle that George was alive. I said nothing about the incident that had almost gotten us killed. I had already told Sahr not to tell anyone. I never went out with him again.

A routine was established: the war raged at night, and we were granted our curfew intermission during the day. The rebels were scattered all over the city, but those who made it to the west of Freetown could not engage because their reinforcements never got past Congo Cross. The president delivered a speech to reassure the public that he had not left the country. The ECOMOG counteroffensive progressed to what they referred to as the "mopping up" stage. They would cordon off a neighborhood and march from house to house, looking for rebels and their collaborators. Civilians in liberated areas also began to attack suspected rebels, who were often simply anyone they had not seen before. This was an irresponsible method of targeting and lynching people at a time when civilians were escaping from other parts of the country and making their way to Freetown. Many innocent people were killed this way.

It took months after the rebels were kicked out of Freetown for the city to regain its life. When it was safe to do so, I rode my bike around town to see the aftermath of the invasion. Stevens Stadium was still full of starving, traumatized, and dying people. Vultures flocked into various parts of the city, monitoring corpses and taking breaks because of overconsumption. There were charred remains of buildings the rebels had burned; walls of buildings where heavy fighting had occurred held evidence of the number of bullets that had been sprayed there. An air of silence remained over the city, but one could hear the melancholic howl of family members mourning their dead relatives. The nauseating smell of stale blood clogged the air in parts of the city where massacres had taken place. Men in protective gear and air masks walked around sections of the city removing human remains for burial and spraying disinfectant. A fear arose that the number of unburied bodies scattered around the city could lead to an outbreak of disease.

The government called on all adults—especially those who were members of uniformed groups such as police, private security, scouts, etc.—to help clean up the city. Young people volunteered to clear the streets and gutters. It was during the cleanup missions that those of us who had survived exchanged information about victims of the latest invasion. We laughed at one of our arrogant neighbors who had been publicly flogged with a thorny branch for violating a curfew. His girlfriend had warned him against going out a few minutes before curfew, but he had boasted that he was above the law. We had all peeped through our windows and watched him wiggle and scream as ECOMOG soldiers brutalized him.

At one point, we were ordered to leave our neighborhoods so the authorities could spray disinfectants. We packed some food and went to Lakka Beach for the day. ECOMOG checkpoints remained all over the city, but residents were free to go about their business without much trouble, except for the long queues at the check-points. When the central government was again functional, to the best of its abilities under the circumstances, schools were ordered to reopen. Many schools in the eastern part of the city had been vandalized, but authorities recognized the importance of getting children back to their classrooms as soon as possible. I was no longer excited about school. My only thought when a new date was announced for SLGS to open was, *Let's just get on with it.*

CHAPTER 14

Sometimes it is not the weight of the kindness
but its timing that touches the heart most.

SLGS was founded on March 25, 1845, by the Church Mis-
sionary Society (CMS) of England. It is the oldest secondary
school in West Africa. I was proud to be a pupil there, but I still
held fears of disappointing my uncle. Though SLGS faced many
resource problems, it was still the most prestigious school in Sierra
Leone, with the smartest students. I made many friends and I was
happy at the school. Pascal was in my grade, and I met Abdo Assad,
who remains my best friend. He was one of the smartest pupils at
SLGS during my time there.

When our first-semester report cards were issued, everyone
expected Abdo to be the top-ranking student of our section, but
when Abdo opened his report card, he discovered that he had been
downgraded. My classmates looked for the person who had out-
ranked Abdo. It was not Selwyn, the other possible candidate. I
remained quiet, and nobody thought of me until someone, I believe
it was Pascal, revealed that I was their new top-ranking pupil. It felt
like I had committed a coup.

When I took my report card home, my uncle was so excited that
he offered to take me out of SLGS and enroll me at Limount College, an expensive private school in Freetown. Auntie Ade, who was
only thinking of how much it would cost her husband to send me
to Limount, replied that the school was meant for "decent children
of rich people." My uncle's suggestion was based on his view that
as a private school, Limount had more resources than SLGS. It was

true at the time, but I had no interest in leaving SLGS for another school. My uncle dropped the matter, but he went around showing my report card to his friends in the neighborhood. He was proud of what I had done, and he started talking about bringing my brother Francis to Freetown, too. Francis arrived a year later and enrolled at SLGS without obstacle. Mariata had her victory against A-Boy, who admitted to underrating me. Oxford, not Carlton Carew, was the new name to take note of at SLGS.

The founding of SLGS is celebrated each year with a Prize Giving and Thanksgiving ceremony in March. Regentonians look forward to these events, and many alumni around the world return to Freetown to attend the celebrations. SLGS students, current and former, are full of pride as they march through Freetown in their well-ironed white pants, white shirts, black blazers, and purple ties; some even accessorize the outfit with felt hats. The ceremonial uniform is expensive, and some parents have to save for months to meet the costs, but no Regentonian parent would deny their child the pride of marching through the streets of Freetown to the rhythm of the Grammar School Band. I enjoyed the Prize Giving and Thanksgiving ceremonies. But my happiest moments were whenever I won a trophy for the school at academic competitions.

I was a member of the SLGS Quiz Team, and I represented the school at many events. On those occasions, I was never reserved about accompanying our acceptance of a trophy with a triumphant singing of the school song. I always felt emotional when we sang in harmony after winning a competition on behalf of the school. My celebrity in Freetown resulted from my many public appearances on behalf of SLGS. Students attended the quiz competitions or listened to them through coverage provided by the Sierra Leone Broadcasting Service (SLBS) radio. Sometimes alumni attended to cheer us on and joined us in singing the "Good Old School" song. An excited alumnus once took my quiz team and all Regentonians present to a downtown restaurant and bought us drinks for winning a tough competition at the Sierra Leone Library Board. When I was alone after a triumphant day at a competition, I sang the third verse of the school song to help me relive the victorious moment:

> When we're marching home in glory, and we've beaten them six–nil
> Or the telegraph's a hundred up, and the captain's batting still;
> When the flag flies for a triumph, that the Good Old School has won
> Then gladly let the chorus rise; and sound it every one.
>
> Live forever, sundered never, faltering never, Grammar School
> Live forever, sundered never, Regentonians true;
> School, school, school, school, school, school,
> God bless our Grammar School.

In those days, when hardly anything provided me with a sense of belonging, the "Grammar School Song" satisfied my feeling of being part of something that was not war. Despite the boyish fights and academic struggles, SLGS succeeded in bestowing upon us a strong sense of brotherhood that was never sundered. Regentonians are always ready to support each other in times of difficulty, at home or abroad. We often salute each other at public gatherings by shouting, "Regentonian!" The SLGS motto is sometimes heard in response: "I pursue!"

My friend Abdo was the only one who knew about my situation at home. He had visited me and witnessed the difficult circumstances in which I lived. My uncle's house was a very old two-story étage with a wooden interior and a corroded zinc roof. The house leaked profusely when it rained, and I had to cover my books with plastic bags and place bowls strategically throughout my room to prevent the water from soaking my bed. Sometimes I would go to bed between bowls of water. I could never prevent all the leaking water from reaching the floor, so when the rain stopped the carpet smelled like a rotten cadaver.

By coincidence, I was reading "Night Rain," a poem by John Pepper Clark, a Nigerian poet, for my West African Secondary School Certificate Examinations (WASSCE). The poem poignantly captures my typical night during the rainy season. After the January 6, 1999, invasion, Mariata encouraged Pascal to come home, and my presence gave him the courage to do so. We shared the same room and bed. Whenever there was heavy rain and we were struggling to contain the water leaking into our room, he would jokingly exclaim, "Oh, night rain!" and then recite lines from the poem:

> What time of night it is
> I do not know
> Except that like some fish
> Doped out of the deep
> I have bobbed up bellywise
> From stream of sleep
> And no cocks crow
> It is drumming hard here
> And I suppose everywhere
> Droning with insistent ardour upon
> Our roof thatch and shed
> And thro' sheaves slit open
> To lightning and rafters
> I cannot quite make out overhead
> Great water drops are dribbling
> Falling like orange or mango . . .

Abdo and I never discussed my situation, but he befriended me, and we shared almost everything: food, clothes, money, textbooks, you name it. He was never afraid of expressing his opinion either to teachers or to his peers. He was the only student who told our math teacher directly that he hated the subject. Almost all the pupils in my arts stream felt the same way, but we never spoke up. Most pupils just did not pay attention during math classes, which made Mrs. Nicol—our math teacher—accuse us of "wasting God's precious time and your fathers' money."

My friendship with Abdo was the beginning of a brotherly love I would forever cherish. Abdo had little to worry about as a pupil in those days—except to outrank me in grades. He made diligent attempts to take my place, but failed each time. When a teacher once asked Abdo why he had let a new student outrank him, he said, "Wae man pass you, e pass you." When a man is greater than you, he is greater than you. My classmates stopped trying to outdo me. That is why they called me Oxford. Almost every SLGS pupil had a nickname based on what others thought suited his character or behavior. Those without nicknames went by their last names. While nicknames like Oxford, Nkrumah, Mandela, or Napoleon were flattering, others like Kaka Teeth (shit teeth), Worwor Face (ugly face), or Gorilla were given to make fun of the bearers. This would constitute bullying in many U.S. schools, but we were brothers and there was no malice involved. Abdo was sometimes called Malata, the Krio version of *mulatto*. Not even the principal, whom we all feared in person, was exempt from the culture of nicknaming. That is how he became Lashor, an affectionate form of his name, Lasite. Mr. Lasite is a Regentonian and might have attained a far worse nickname during his high school days, but none among us was brave enough to investigate the matter. Although Mr. Lasite is a tough disciplinarian, Regentonians love and respect him for his commitment to the school's prestige and high academic standards.

The quest to know the secret behind my success at SLGS led Abdo to my house and brought him face to face with the reality of my life. But like most compassionate people, he stayed. We became brothers and cotroublemakers. Though I cannot vouch, in true Regentonian spirit, that we were "souls that never were mean," I have no doubt we were "hearts that never quailed at need."

CHAPTER 15

Our youth is the advantage
we have to make the
world a better place.

When we were not doing homework or holding intense political debates about the war, Abdo and I visited girls we liked. It was easy for me to charm the girls with my prestigious SLGS prefect badge. My position created an imbalance between Abdo and me, because he wanted to attract girls more than I did. Abdo also knew that I had a crush on his sister, Loris.

"So, fellow," Abdo said to me one day when we were on our way to Annie Walsh, the female counterpart of SLGS, "you don't really need that badge to be a prefect. Everyone knows who you are, and you attract girls anyway. I will take your badge whenever we go out, so I can be a prefect, too."

"What?! Lashor will kill me!" I said. Whether on or off campus, Regentonians are expected to uphold the integrity of the school.

"Forget Lashor! He won't know. But you know what, my sister will know, and that's a promotion for you." He was making fun of my crush on Loris.

"Who says I want your white girl?" I replied with laughter.

"Well, if you don't mind, I will tell Loris what you just said."

Abdo knew I wouldn't want Loris to hear that. Sarcastic comments on whiteness were not nice to girls who were naturally light-skinned. Black girls had started using chemical lotions to make their skin lighter. We called them Washie-Worwor. A side effect of bleaching is that the skin quickly gets black burns from the sun in the body's attempts to repair itself. It is the camouflage appearance of the burned skin that earned the name Washie-Worwor.

"All right, don't tell Loris. Take the badge."

I gave Abdo my badge, and he became a prefect among girls he liked. Sometimes I slipped up and told people that he wasn't a prefect, but I would quickly retract my statement to restore his prestige. I never got my badge back from Abdo, but I was happy that it made him what he wanted to be at the time: popular and charming. It has become our tradition that I ask him to return my prefect badge every time I see him.

Like me, Abdo lived with his uncle. He used to share his lunch with me and tell me stories of how proud his uncle was of his grades. Abdo was working hard toward the WASSCE, a nightmare that awaits every Sierra Leonean student who wishes to enter college. Abdo's uncle had promised to send him to school in the U.S. or U.K. if he kept his side of the deal by getting excellent grades on the exam. As for me, the exam was going to be the end of my affordable education. Though I had no idea what would happen after the WASSCE, I was happy to have made it this far in school.

One incident almost prevented me from taking the WASSCE. In 2001, SLGS prefects were concerned about encroachments on school property. Several residents of Freetown had illegally purchased parts of the school's land and constructed houses. The prefects were informed that the court had ruled the encroachment illegal in the early 1990s, but by 2000 construction of illegal houses had increased, even close to campus. The prefects met to discuss the issue and perhaps call on the Old Boys Union (SLGS Alumni Association) to trigger an enforcement of the existing court ruling.

Before we could meet again, word spread among the illegal tenants that we were planning a raid on their houses. I was stationed outside the school building the following morning to assist with punishing latecomers, students who arrived after morning devotion had started. It was Ash Wednesday, so it was particularly important that stragglers not interrupt the service. Many students were late that morning, and they stood outside, awaiting their punishment. Illegal tenants who had received information about our meeting the previous day assumed that the students were mobilizing to attack them. They began to throw stones at us, and before I could tell the students to move away and not respond, they had descended on the tenants in full force, releasing a volley of stones in return. Mr. Lasite came outside, followed by those in the auditorium. The campus had suddenly become a war zone of students with ash crosses on their foreheads, like members of a cult, against a group of illegal tenants. I joined Mr. Lasite downhill as we attempted in vain to get the students to retreat.

In a few minutes, forces from the United Nations Armed Mission to Sierra Leone (UNAMSIL), who had gradually taken over security in Freetown, arrived. Military helicopters hovered overhead, and SLGS became news on FM stations. The peacekeepers deployed and ordered students off campus. They were marched to Congo Cross in groups. The government acted swiftly because dormant AFRC/RUF rebels in the city could have easily hijacked such an incident. When the last group of boys left campus, I walked home with the remaining peacekeepers. SLGS was closed indefinitely. When my uncle heard about the riot on the radio, he drove up the hill to get Francis and me, but we were both in the middle of the crossfire, assisting Mr. Lasite. Francis was also a prefect.

Some days after the riot, I was studying at home when I heard a knock at the door. I came out wearing flip-flops, shorts, and a T-shirt. I was arrested and placed in the back of a military police van without any warrant or charges. I was driven to a police station, an unfinished building, at King Jimmy wharf, and thrown in a cell—a dungeon. It was worse than my cell in Voinjama. It was overcrowded with young prisoners, pushing and pulling each other for a chance to inhale some fresh air through the metal bars on the upper part of the door. They begged visitors for water or food through the same hole. The gaseous smell coming from the shit and piss in an open bucket shared by the prisoners could have operated a generator. Many, like me, had been detained without formal charges or information about why they were there.

I found a corner close to the door, where I could receive a bit of air, and stood there for the whole day, resisting every push or pull. Later that evening, the prison door opened and an officer said my name. Auntie Ade and Mr. Lasite had arrived. This is when I realized that I had been arrested because of the SLGS riot. Mr. Lasite brought lawyers with him. A couple of them were Regentonians, wearing the school tie. I was taken from the cell to the Criminal Investigation Department headquarters, where Mr. Lasite, Auntie Ade, and the lawyers were waiting. When I saw the many lawyers who had come to set me free, I was proud to be a Regentonian. I made a statement to the police in the presence of my lawyers, and Mr. Lasite drove me and my aunt home. It was my first time to enter his infamous Lada car. He had held onto that Lada for so long that it became known locally as Lasite Lada.

A few days later, I returned for criminal identification, but the case was dismissed, and an order for the enforcement of the existing ruling was granted. During a hilarious turn of events, a tenant was asked whether she could identify any of the pupils who threw stones at her. She assertively pointed at Mr. Lasite until she was informed that he was the principal. Everyone laughed and she walked away in embarrassment.

My classmates never heard about my arrest and imprisonment. If they had, I would have most certainly become "Oxford the Prisoner." I returned home from Norway one summer, and the illegal buildings had been demolished and a fence constructed around the school.

After the WASSCE, there was nothing to do but wait for the results. My uncle was happy that I had graduated so he wouldn't have to worry about my school fees anymore. Things had gotten tougher when his minivan broke down and he was jobless. His French partners in the hotel business decided Sierra Leone was no longer a viable business location and did not return to the country.

I purchased a Yashica camera that I used to make money as a photographer. Mainly, I took photographs of Abdo for his girlfriends. For every flattering picture of him, he paid me double our agreed-upon price. My camera was pretty sophisticated for the time, so taking great pictures wasn't a huge challenge. Whenever Abdo loved a photo, he asked for multiple copies, for which I charged more. Abdo's mother was living in the Gambia, so we sent some of the pictures to her. I made a significant income from taking photos of my schoolmates.

I also befriended the blind students at SLGS. They resided at the Milton Margai School for the Blind and were a grade below me. I grew close to Joseph Abdulai, who was very sharp. When he entered a room, he could distinguish my cologne from a wave of boys' cologne. He could also tell by shaking my right hand if I had forgotten my watch, which I wore on my left wrist.

The students at the school for the blind were taught Braille, but since there were no Braille textbooks, they relied on voice recorders they carried to classes. I was their voiceover man. On weekends, I recorded textbook materials on cassette tapes for Joseph, and he shared them with his friends. Sometimes I rode my bike down Wilkinson Road, toward Lumley, to deliver the recorder to their school. When I graduated from SLGS, the responsibility went to Francis.

I usually held Joseph's hand when we walked together. One day, I told him that a girl he liked was walking toward us. He immediately told me to let go of his hand so he could pretend that he wasn't blind. I gave him a friendly reminder that he would be fooling no one. I refused to let go of his hand because it was during the rainy season and there were puddles everywhere. Joseph and I remained close friends until I graduated. I saw him a couple of times at Fourah Bay College, where he enrolled after SLGS.

CHAPTER 16

Life shared, even under the most difficult conditions,
creates a meaningful bond between
those who experience it.

After sitting for my WASSCE in 2001, and with nothing to do in Freetown, I returned to Guinea to visit my mother. She was living in Kountaya Refugee Camp, where she had been relocated after rebels from Liberia and Sierra Leone, with support from Charles Taylor, invaded Gueckedou in 2000. Guinea was the latest casualty of Taylor's attempt to destabilize the Mano River Union. Many of my old friends escaped from Gueckedou and made it to Freetown, where they stayed with us at my uncle's house for a while. My cousin Kendema was one of those who came to Freetown. UNHCR relocated many of the refugees in Gueckedou prefecture to Kountaya. It was the first time I visited my mother there. Conditions were always the same in all new refugee camps: starvation, disease, and desperation. Some refugees wanted to return to Sierra Leone immediately after Tejan Kabbah's return to power in 1998, but that dream was shattered by the January 1999 invasion of Freetown.

Sierra Leonean refugees in Guinea were always excited when someone returned from their country. To a refugee or anyone stranded behind conflict lines, a visitor from home is like an angel, even if he or she bears bad news. Such visits were their only means of receiving credible information about family and friends. They were also eager to know whether it was safe to return home. Many of them were tired of living in the isolated jungle in which the UN had placed them. They called the camp Leh Camp because of the high number of bush pigs that inhabited the area (*leh* is Mandingo for *bush pig*). I called it the United Nations Republic of Kountaya, which made my mother laugh. I could understand their anxiety; it had taken me three days to catch the only public transportation from Kissidougou, the main provincial town, to the camp. The minivan, known as Ma Kpana or Grandma Kpana, broke down at least five times before we reached Kountaya. I was covered in dust from head to toe, as though I had just been resurrected.

The refugees were living away from civilization, separated from angry Guineans who blamed them for the attack on their country. Taylor's action had forced the refugees out of their own countries; now he had turned them into targets in their land of refuge. I found life in Kountaya very difficult, but many of those who lived there had quickly learned to adapt after many years of moving from camp to camp. I was happy to see my mother after such a long time. I had feared for her life when I heard news of the rebel attack on Gueckedou. Survivors who made it to Freetown informed me that the Bambo compound had been bombed. No one had seen my mother or the other members of my family. My sister Hawa was still in Conakry when the attack took place.

After a week of living with my mother, I returned to Kissidougou, where Hawa was working with a German organization called GTZ. Because Kissidougou is the closest prefecture to Kountaya, many of the NGOs working in the refugee camps had moved their headquarters there. I met several people I knew from Gueckedou. Some of them were working for NGOs assisting other refugees in Kountaya. I had nothing to do in Kissidougou except to stay home and read when my sister was at work. It was a good opportunity for me to refresh my Kissi and Mandingo. I also took evening computer classes at the Blue Chip Computer Center, a computer café that belonged to my friend Barry, who now worked for IRC. I had no computer skills, but Word and Excel seemed easy. I sometimes helped with the Professional English classes. Barry and I used to reminisce about our time in Gueckedou. Life shared, even under the most difficult conditions, leaves a meaningful bond between those who experience it.

After several weeks of living between Kountaya Camp and Kissidougou, I obtained an IRC scholarship grant to study computer science at the École des Études et de Scolarité in Conakry. My mother, who wasn't sure that I would accept the award, was very happy when I decided to give it a try. She had asked if I wanted to take a job in the refugee camp, like most of my friends had done, but I told her that I was not ready for such a commitment. I wanted to go to college!

CHAPTER 17

Dangerous is one who believes himself
at war with others when all along he
has only himself to conquer.

I moved to Conakry in September 2001 after passing the IRC exam for a scholarship grant. I thought living there would provide an opportunity for me to pursue a UN scholarship to further my studies. The UN sometimes gave individual study-abroad scholarships to students who did well in the IRC school system. I lived with Mama Yawa in Hamdallaye. Every morning, I walked up to Aéroport, where my computer institute was located. The school was not very challenging, so I became eager to finish the program and find something better. We were supposed to be learning computer science in a school where there were about a dozen computers for some two hundred students working toward their Brevet de Technicien Supérieur (Higher Technical Education Certificate). Only about four of the computers worked properly at any given time. Sometimes there was no electricity to run the facility, and the generator was a piece of crap. My French, however, improved during my short stay in Conakry. It was also an opportunity for me to spend time with my younger sister Amie. She had been living with Mama Yawa since our father's death.

By 2001, Conakry had become a hostile place for Sierra Leoneans and Liberians. The attack on Gueckedou and Macenta prefectures had created resentment toward refugees in Guinea. Refugees were often subject to police brutality and harassment. Mama Yawa told me to always return home as soon as school was over, although my situation was better than that of many refugees because I spoke French and held a Guinean student ID. I attended a short course at a local school that qualified me for a *carte scolaire*. Mama Yawa also took me to the local chief, who gave me a certificate of domicile. Whenever the police stopped me for an ID, I produced my *carte scolaire* and answered their questions in French or Mandingo. When I traveled around Guinea, I was usually exempted from harassment because of my *carte scolaire*.

I sometimes spent my afternoons with Sia Tolno, my uncle Sahr J's second daughter, who lived in Conakry and worked as a musician. Sia and I studied French together when we weren't talking about Auntie Ade and her antics. Sia never tired of recounting stories of her own days of abuse and deprivation in Freetown. Sometimes she laughed at the absurdity of the maltreatment she had endured as a child, and it was difficult for me to distinguish her pain from the natural sense of humor that runs in our family. I wondered whether she was really laughing or simply suppressing her pain. Laughter is sometimes a coping mechanism for dealing with bad memories. To laugh at the horror of one's past can mitigate the agony of it.

When I wasn't with Sia, I spent time listening to Mama Lobou, my mother's aunt, who was temporarily living with Mama Yawa for medical care. Mama Lobou is originally from Tomadou, a village on the Guinea–Sierra Leone border. She had raised my mother and her siblings after their mother passed away. They called her "mother." She hated everything to do with modernity, including pills. Mama Yawa had gone through hell to get her to Conakry for medical care. Mama Lobou detested traveling in vehicles. She had to be cajoled like a child every morning to take her medication. But Mama Lobou was very knowledgeable in herbal medicine and traditional healing. She sometimes translated the sounds of birds and insects and walked around the compound looking for useful herbs among the flowers and weeds. Mama Lobou was highly respected among Kissi people because she was the sister of Chief Bandabla, one of the greatest chiefs of Tomadou, and she was active in the Toma, female circumcision society.

The life of Chief Bandabla was centered in mystery. There were rumors that the sun had gone down early on the day he died, and many people had seen his ghost walk up a rocky mountain close to Tomadou. When the ghost disappeared after a squeaky sound originated from the rock, Bandabla breathed his last breath. I tried to confirm the stories with Mama Lobou, but her only response was that her brother had been a great man. Everyone who knew Mama Lobou referred to her in Kissi as *yema masaa*, sister of a chief. Despite her hatred of modernity, she was a believer in Western education. The easiest way for a grandchild to get anything from Mama Lobou was to do well in school. She refused to talk to any of her grandchildren who did not take school seriously. Mama Lobou loved Sahr J more than her other children, but she was angry with him too. She blamed him for allowing his wife to abuse his children.

Even when she was extremely bothered, Mama Lobou was good at internalizing her anger. She would refuse to talk for days when she was troubled. She was also a prayerful person, but I never saw her attend church or mosque—though she prayed and offered libations to the ancestors on behalf of her grandchildren, especially those who were far away from her. She gave me lessons on things I should not do with respect to my Kissi customs and heritage, and "as a man." When I was in Conakry, she rarely ate without me. Every school day, she recited her blessings for me long after I said good-bye in the morning. Rumor had it that Mama Lobou had a hidden financial reserve in the event that one of her grandchildren ever got in trouble and needed money. I know she carried a *bouyee* under her wrapper that she took off only when she was absolutely certain no one was around. It was one of the reasons she turned down Mama Yawa's offers to help her bathe, even when she was too sick to do it herself: she imagined her daughter might take her money.

When Mama Lobou wanted to give me money, she pulled me into a corner, shifted her wrapper to the side, and unzipped her *bouyee*. She quickly placed the money in my hand and told me to go. She didn't want her other grandchildren to see that she was giving me money. It was obvious, though, that I was one of her favorite grandchildren. When she received even a piece of cake in my absence, she kept half for me. She believed that a student should never be hungry. But Mama Lobou was what we call *get nah an* in Krio—grumpy—everything involving her had to be done the hard way. When Mama Yawa wanted her to do something, like take her medication, put on her slippers, or shower, I was the messenger, one of the few people who could get through to her. She wanted to return to Tomadou, but Mama Yawa rejected her requests until she was well. I believe she often refused to do certain things to annoy her daughter into sending her back to her village, for whatever reason.

While in Conakry, I looked forward to news of my WASSCE results. I had no specific plans other than returning to Freetown as soon as the results were released. My performance on the WASSCE could determine my next option. It was difficult to catch Sierra Leone radio frequencies in Conakry, but I was sometimes lucky at night. I tuned my radio to SLBS every evening, hoping to hear news about WASSCE results. Unfortunately, and for some bizarre reason, the only things that came through clearly on my radio were SLBS obituaries. Everything else was fuzzy most of the time.

CHAPTER 18

There is no toolbox for making the world a
better place. One must simply render what
random act of kindness, what community duty,
what humble service is within his means
toward shaping a peaceful world.

In December 2001, Mariata and Pascal came to Conakry for the
holidays. I had gotten very good WASSCE marks. I decided to
complete my first year at the institute before returning to Freetown. It was a two-year program. Pascal informed me that my
WASSCE marks made me eligible for a government grant to study
at Fourah Bay College. I had done well in all nine subjects; not
only that, but remarkably I was one of a small number of students who passed both English and math. In Sierra Leone, just as
arts stream students do not take math seriously, science students
ignore English. I always thought each subject was as relevant as
the other, even when I struggled with math. I never gave up on
any subject because it was difficult; rather, I devoted more time
and attention to it. When math proved difficult, I studied more
math. My efforts didn't always lead to wonderful results, but not
for a lack of trying.

In March 2002, the month of SLGS Prize Giving and Thanksgiving ceremonies, I returned to Freetown after a risky journey in a
trawler that almost ended up sinking. Sierra Leoneans are afraid of
the sea, but the dangers of bad roads and rebel kidnappings—even
after the war was declared over—made journeying by sea safer. I had
traveled by the same trawler en route to Guinea after my WASSCE.

The trawler, like all public transportation in Sierra Leone, Guinea, and Liberia, loaded more passengers than was officially allowed. Traders, diplomats, general passengers, and children crowded the trawler. We jostled against and sprawled across one another, puking and groaning like creatures under an evil spell. Bags upon bags of vomit flew out the windows as we floundered across the ocean in the belly of our unsafe vessel.

I do not get seasick, so I volunteered to hold babies whose mothers were throwing up, to offer water or more plastic bags to others, or to hold back the clothes of violent pukers. I sometimes took a break from nursing and went on deck to hang out with the crew. When my fellow passengers were tired of puking their guts out, they reclined in their seats like lifeless objects, swinging from side to side, back and forth, with the movement of the trawler. After hours of passengers puking, the trawler was suffused with a sticky smell of human gas and whatever rotten goods were onboard. There were times when I thought we might die, as the boat was thrown by waves and water came gushing in. Christians onboard said the Lord's Prayer, and Muslims recited the *fatir*. Children cried, not because they were afraid of dying, but because they were hungry for more breast milk from their nauseated mothers. When we made it to Freetown and the trawler docked smoothly, passengers clapped, perhaps in gratitude to their god for saving us, as battered as we were by the roughness of our voyage.

WASSCE results were still a topic of conversation among schoolboys and schoolgirls in Freetown. Students and teachers debated the names of the best candidates. Some candidates were well known to their peers even before the exams, and students often measured their own performances by the grades of the best candidates. I was one of the students people looked to for such affirmation, because I was Oxford. If students like me performed poorly on the exam, those who failed could justify their bad performances by claiming that the exam was particularly difficult.

My absence from Freetown led to speculation that I had already gone to Europe to study. Some people assumed I wouldn't be at the SLGS Prize Giving ceremony to receive my awards. I was excited, but I held myself together until I arrived at the campus. I saw Abdo, who had also returned from vacation to attend the ceremony. I spent the evening receiving prizes with other students amid public applause, as the Regentonian band played a hymn I knew well:

> One more step along the world I go,
> one more step along the world I go;
> from the old things to the new,
> keep me traveling along with you.
>
> And it's from the old I travel to the new;
> keep me traveling along with you.
>
> Round the corners of the world I turn,
> more and more about the world I learn;
> all the new things that I see
> you'll be looking at along with me.
>
> And it's from the old I travel to the new;
> keep me traveling along with you.
>
> As I travel through the bad and good,
> keep me traveling the way I should;
> where I see no way to go
> you'll be telling me the way I know.
>
> And it's from the old I travel to the new;
> keep me traveling along with you.

Give me courage when the world is rough,
keep me loving though the world is tough;
leap and sing in all I do,
keep me traveling along with you.

And it's from the old I travel to the new;
keep me traveling along with you.

You are older than the world can be,
you are younger than the life in me;
ever old and ever new,
keep me traveling along with you.

After the ceremony, I met a former classmate who told me about a UWC (United World College) scholarship program. He was disappointed that he had not seen me earlier. I had never heard of the UWCs, even though another Regentonian I knew, Leonard Gordon, was attending the school in Norway. I met with Mr. Lasite, who confirmed the information. However, the deadline to apply had passed. I could have shrugged and moved on with my life, but I would have never been satisfied, knowing that I should have at least tried. I decided to find whoever was in charge of the UWC program and attempt to apply. Whether I would be accepted or not did not matter. I just wanted to be considered.

The following morning, I went to see Ms. Jones, who worked at the Ministry of Education and was in charge of the UWC program. I presented my documents to her. She proceeded to scold me like an angry mother for being late. But she also admitted that she had wondered why I hadn't applied. Her position made her aware of the likely candidates based on WASSCE results. I had also brought a note from Mr. Lasite. She was impressed that he would write a note on my behalf. When Ms. Jones looked through my academic records, she put her earlier frustration aside and started to speak French to me. She had noticed French among my nine WASSCE subjects. I answered *oui* or *non* to her multiple questions. She wondered why she had never seen me at Alliance Française, the French cultural center.

Ms. Jones invited me to a panel interview at the Ministry of Education, scheduled for a few days later. There were four or five people on the panel. Ms. Jones made a presentation about the UWCs, after which the panelists asked me questions in order to determine my eligibility. I answered them sincerely, with no desire to say more or less than necessary. I had felt a connection to Ms. Jones, and she seemed honest, but I held doubts about the ministry. In those days, such scholarships were for sale, and I had no money to bribe anyone. Many promising students had their hopes for government and international scholarships dashed at the ministry, and I was afraid of raising mine too high.

At the end of the interview, Ms. Jones asked which UWC I preferred. My options were Canada, India, Singapore, and Norway. I chose the country I knew only by name and nothing else: Norway. I knew about Canada, because when I was a refugee in Guinea we received Kellogg's Corn Flakes with pictures of track-and-field legend Donovan Bailey on the boxes. Even *enfants maigres réfugiés* like us dreamed of becoming Donovan. Bollywood taught me about India, but more importantly, we had a large contingent of Indian UN peacekeepers in the country. I learned about Singapore when I represented SLGS in quiz competitions. Ms. Jones looked satisfied that I'd chosen Norway. Other applicants were more interested in Canada. I later learned that RCNUWC is Ms. Jones' favorite UWC school.

That night, I discovered Norway in a geography book. Francis found it funny that I would choose what he called a "fridge." He joked that Africans who go to Norway turn into ice statues outside the Oslo airport. I couldn't help but join his laughter. I knew he was happy for me, but we never let each other get away without a little brotherly deprecating humor. He was sure that the scholarship program wasn't another government scam to scrape money out of poor people. We decided that I would stay in Freetown and pursue the scholarship, and he would travel to Guinea to inform the family about my new plan.

I passed the interview for RCNUWC. A few weeks later, I received an acceptance folder from Norway. I was happy, but I had little money to meet the financial requirements of the scholarship. My uncle sold everything of value he owned to assist me, even though he was skeptical that the scholarship might be a scam. When corruption becomes rampant in a government, citizens can no longer expect anything for free. Ms. Jones was only responsible for selecting qualified students and recommending them to the various UWCs. Each student was in charge of making his own travel arrangements. The reason Ms. Jones was glad that I'd chosen Norway was because RCNUWC is one of the few schools that offer full scholarships, including travel fare, to Sierra Leoneans. I was, however, responsible for obtaining a visa to Norway, which was not easy. The Norwegian representation in Freetown was a small consulate that did not issue visas.

The Norwegian consulate was located near the Leocem Cement Factory in Cline Town, east of Freetown. I had limited funds, and my bicycle was no longer working, so I walked from Murray Town to Cline Town for my visa application. Sometimes I walked there only to be told that no new information was available from Abidjan, Ivory Coast, where the nearest embassy was located. I had walked there in vain so many times that the young Sierra Leonean woman in charge felt sorry for me. I decided to have fun with the situation and used it to explore Freetown. I went through neighborhoods and visited places I had never seen before. Those journeys on foot between Cline Town and Murray Town exposed me to the damage Freetown had endured in 1999 and the wretched lives many people led in the ruined city.

In my view, the entire Fourah Bay Road area, which I had to pass through to get to the consulate, was a health hazard. People lived in partially burned houses covered only with cardboard and rusty zinc panels. The sewers were full of excrement, filth, and dead animals. There may even have been decomposed human bodies in some of the gutters. The streets were congested with people walking aimlessly. It took more than an hour to get through the crowd. Vehicles, motorbikes, bicycles, *amolankes* (pushcarts), and humans competed for narrow roads.

I window-shopped in downtown Freetown as though I intended to make big purchases. This was how I kept myself up to date on new technology. In 2002, Nokia cell phones were just arriving in the country. I went through Kroo Bay, where man and swine competed for the same putrefied space. I saw children defecating in a stream, pigs feeding downstream, and children drawing water from the same stream that runs through the slum. Unfortunately, this state of affairs remains unchanged to this day.

I went through Congo Town, passing over the Congo Town Bridge, which crosses the Congo River. The choking smoke perpetually rising from the garbage depository there compelled a faster pace. When new trucks full of Freetown's rubbish arrived, naked children hastened to scavenge through the waste for whatever could be recycled in their disadvantaged lives. I enjoyed hearing the rhythm from the anvils of blacksmiths and other metalsmiths, who constructed hoes, cutlasses, pots, doors, and so forth on the bank of the river. Alongside the smiths were loggers who sold the planks needed for the makeshift reconstruction of Freetown. Sometimes I took a break on Wilkinson Road to see my friends the Bainda family. From the Bainda residence, I took the back roads of Cole Farm and made my way to Andrew Street.

"How is it?" my uncle always asked.

"They said I should come back next week."

I made those trips for weeks. Finally, I was told that it would be best if I simply went to Abidjan. By waiting in Freetown, it was unlikely that I would receive my visa in time to travel. My airplane

ticket arrived from Norway, but I still lacked a visa. The school sent
brochures that I enjoyed reading. The beauty of the campus and
the happy faces of young people inspired me. When I informed
Ms. Jones about my problems obtaining a visa, we came up with
the idea that I should modify my flight to allow me to have a layover
in Abidjan. It was a great plan, but I had no money, and changing
my flight also meant a layover in Dakar, Senegal. But in the end it
was my best option for getting to Norway, so I decided to pursue it
despite the disadvantages.

Ms. Jones introduced me to a Sierra Leone government official
who had relatives in Abidjan. He promised to lodge me with his
family, but a few days before my departure he told me that his family was unable to host me. I have no idea what had changed, and I
had no time to look for alternative lodging, so I decided to fly to
Abidjan without any housing arrangement. I did not inform my
uncle or Ms. Jones about the change of plan. Before I left, my uncle
sold a new cell phone he had received from a friend in Europe and
gave me forty U.S. dollars. I had another fifty thousand leones for
the journey. I packed a few clothes and a couple of books in a small
suitcase. On August 25, 2002, my uncle accompanied me to Lungi
International Airport, where I boarded a Concorde to Abidjan via
Conakry. It was my first time on a plane, but it felt like I had flown
before. I was unsure how I was going to find a place to stay in Abidjan, but I was not worried. I was determined to leave Freetown.

We landed at Félix-Houphouët-Boigny International a few hours
after a brief stopover in Conakry. Ivory Coast is an ECOWAS state,
so I walked through customs without difficulty. It also helped that
I speak French. Instead of rushing outside, I sat in the airport
arrival lobby for a while, pretending I was waiting for someone to
pick me up. I had no plan, so I wanted to observe the atmosphere
and read the billboards; perhaps I could find a room for twenty

dollars. In those days, one could find a motel room in Freetown for that amount, and I was hoping Abidjan wasn't too different. I watched as joyful family members embraced their newly arrived relatives and left. Gradually, the population at the airport decreased, and the hustlers began to leave. This was the moment I decided to exit the airport and try to find out whether there were any cheap motels nearby.

As soon as I stepped outside the lobby, a man who was obviously Nigerian approached me. He recommended hotels for a commission and helped confused visitors for a fee. I told him that I needed somewhere cheap to stay. His understanding of cheap was all the high-rated hotels he proceeded to list for me. Those were the places he received his commissions from. When he was done, I told him in Nigerian pidgin that I meant somewhere a poor boy could crash for a night. He understood and recommended a cheap motel on one of the beaches of Abidjan. He warned me that it was very basic, but it offered the lowest price anywhere in the city. I also informed him that I was in Abidjan to apply for a Norwegian visa, but I didn't know anyone in town. He volunteered to accompany me to the embassy the following day. I made it clear to him that I had very little money.

"My friend, mek you nor worry, no problem," he said and took my little suitcase.

We drove to a motel not too far from the airport. I checked into a small room that, as the Nigerian man had accurately informed me, held only the basics: bed, shower, table, and chair.

I took a quick shower and lay down on the bed to think. Just as I was about to fall asleep, I heard a knock. I opened the door and saw my Nigerian friend standing there with four beautiful young ladies. He wanted to know whether I was interested in some fun. I didn't know what to say in my confused state, but I told him that I was in the middle of something and he should come back. I went to bed and did not wake up until the next morning.

We took a taxi to the Norwegian embassy, which was located in Plateau, a picturesque quarter of Abidjan. I had never seen an African city as pretty and clean as Abidjan. There was no litter in Plateau, and the streets looked like those of the Western cities I had seen in movies. It made me reflect on the poor state of Freetown, but I concluded that our civil war was to blame. Sadly, however, Freetown still has made no significant improvement since the end of the war.

We arrived at the embassy around 7:45 a.m. and waited till nine. I had already paid the visa fee at the consulate in Freetown. I simply needed to present my passport and answer some questions. The consular agent told me that my visa could be ready in a week. I replied that I needed the visa that same day because I had a flight to Dakar that evening. I was already late for school. She looked through my flight tickets and realized that I was telling the truth. Without further trouble, she said to come back at four p.m. It would have cost more money to return to the motel, so we found a shady area close to the embassy and sat there until my visa was ready. I wondered why it had taken them so long to issue the visa while I was in Freetown, but it no longer mattered.

We returned to the motel to grab my suitcase and head to the airport. I gave the Nigerian man twenty U.S. dollars and fifty thousand leones as payment for the motel and his services. He insisted that I give him more money. I showed him my remaining twenty dollars and told him it was all I had for my one-night transit in Dakar. He would not believe that I was traveling to Norway without much money.

"Nor be poor man dae come go Europe like that." Poor people do not travel to Europe like that. "My friend, mek you go at least top this thing to one hundred dollars. This fifty thousand leones be shit money." I could not contest that last bit. The leones were worth very little in Ivory Coast.

I was still pleading with him when the last call for my flight was announced. I left him and went through security, wishing I had enough money to pay him for the enormous assistance he rendered to me. I don't know what I would have done without him, but I hoped he understood my predicament. He had assumed that I was only trying to conceal my wealth when I told him I needed a cheap place to stay. His suspicion was heightened by the fact that I walked into an embassy and received a visa the same day. In his mind, no ordinary African could pull such a stunt. Little did he know that I had been corresponding with the embassy for weeks, walking from one end of Freetown to the other on an empty stomach. Sometimes we see only the surface tales of other people's stories. I did not just waltz into a Norwegian embassy and obtain a visa; it had required weeks of tango.

On August 26, 2002, I arrived at Léopold Sédar Senghor International in Dakar with my remaining twenty dollars in my pocket. When I walked out of the airport, I was immediately surrounded by a group of five boys advertising hotels. I told them I did not have enough money to stay at any of the hotels they were advertising, but I was desperately in need of a cheap place to stay.

"Tu as combien?"—how much money do you have?—they asked in French.

"Bon, je n'ai pas plus de vingt dollars." I don't have more than twenty dollars.

They looked at each other, and I could tell they didn't believe me. After realizing that I was dead serious, they told me that my cheapest option would be to stay with them and give them the money. I accepted the offer. We boarded a minivan and went to their residence in the heart of Dakar. I was nervous, but I remained calm on the surface. I was worth twenty dollars and a suitcase full of worn-out clothes.

After a short drive, we arrived at their residence, a series of modest mud houses in a compound. They took me from room to room, corner to corner, to shake hands with everyone—old, young, male, and female relatives. I felt like a long-lost family member who had found his way home. It was night, so the women were cooking multiple pots of food for dinner. The children ran around, fetching condiments and dishes. After I had met everyone, the boys took me to a small back room, which evidently was their bedroom. One of them spread a prayer mat in front of the bed.

"Mon ami, c'est ton lit ça." My friend, this is your bed.

I nodded in affirmation, and we walked out together. They offered me a small bowl of *lafidi*, rice sprinkled with pepper and palm oil. I ate the food while they asked questions about Sierra Leone and my journey to Norway. They were impressed that I was traveling to Norway on a scholarship. They called one of their teenage sisters and suggested that I marry her. I said I had a wife in Freetown.

"Alors, elle sera ta deuxième femme." Then she will become your second wife.

We laughed. The girl ran back to the kitchen.

I slept little that night, but I was grateful for the gift of a mat on a floor below four snoring boys. The following morning, the five boys took me to the SN Brussels office in Dakar. Since I'd changed my flight to spend a day in Abidjan, I needed a new ticket from Dakar to Brussels. Nowadays such changes would require an exorbitant fee, but in those days I paid nothing. When my new ticket was booked, we walked around Dakar, which is a beautiful city. I thought of Léopold Sédar Senghor, the first president of Senegal, who was also one of Africa's finest intellectuals. He is sometimes mocked as spending more time writing poems than leading his country. He was one of the founders of the *négritude*, a black intellectual movement described by Aimé Césaire as the simple recognition of the fact that one is black. Senghor was the first African to be elected to the Académie Française—a French club of forty members who hold authority on the French language and its evolution. Its members are referred to as Les Immortels, the immortals. I learned about Senghor because he was one of My Lord's favorite poets. My favorite Senghor poem is "Femme Noire" (Black Woman), which is the only poem I love to read in French. I would later write a college paper on the *négritude* philosophy.

In the afternoon, we took a minivan to a quarter near the airport, where we spent the rest of the day. Here, too, I was introduced to every family member. I had barely slept the night before, so I tried to nap until we were ready to go to the airport, but my hosts kept asking questions about my trip. They seemed genuinely fascinated by my opportunity. I politely answered their questions. The family reminded me of my own, and that gave me the patience to accommodate their curiosity.

When it was time, we drove to the airport. I gave the boys the twenty dollars and thanked them for their help. They accepted my gratitude, recited some Islamic blessings, and graciously asked for more. I told them that it was all the money I had, but they did not believe me, except the fellow who appeared to be the oldest among them. They insisted on more money, but he said something in Wolof, which I think was an instruction that they should leave me alone, because after he said it, no more demands were made for money. I looked at him, and he indicated with a hand gesture that I should go and check in. I looked each of them in the eye and said *merci*. They nodded and replied *bon voyage*.

I went through check-in and made it to the gate. It was a late-night flight, so I had a few hours to kill. Everything seemed unbelievable to me until I boarded the flight to Brussels. It was incredible that there were no more obstacles on my way to Norway, a new beginning. When I fastened my seatbelt, placed my seat in an upright position, and the plane took off, my mind wandered to the misfortunes and fortunes of my life, the chances I had taken, and the lingering question of God. I reflected on whom I should condemn for my tribulations and whom I should thank for my blessings. If

God was my guide, why did I have to go through so much trouble? If it wasn't God, then who had sent those earthly angels who had helped me along the way? Perhaps that is the nature of man, to be good. But for the moment, I answered "chicken" to the question "Chicken or beef?"

CHAPTER 19

Wind may force a coconut tree to bend this way and that, but does nothing to its roots.

In August 2004, after failing to get a U.S. visa in Norway, I arrived back in Freetown. My plan was to proceed to Conakry to reapply for a U.S. visa there. I was happy to be home, to see my brother and uncle again. But I had little time to waste; I needed to travel to the U.S. in time for the start of the academic year. A few days later, I left Freetown for Conakry. It was great to see my mother, who was visiting Mama Yawa. I also enjoyed being reunited with Amie, my cousins, and other family members and friends in Hamdallaye. A trip to Europe is a prideful achievement in the eyes of many Guineans. My mother's relatives stopped by to congratulate me. Their best wishes made me glad, but I hated the underlying implication that a journey to Europe was a fundamental accomplishment. It is this portrayal of Europe that forces Africans to attempt to get there by any means possible. Africans continue to drown between North Africa and Europe because they believe Europe is full of unlimited opportunities.

I was happy to see my mother. The last time I'd seen her, she had been trying to get settled in Kountaya Camp. I would not have had the time to visit her there, where she was now head of a refugee technical-training institute. I recounted stories of my time in Norway, people I'd met, and my opportunity to go to the United States. My family listened keenly and burst into celebration when I informed them about my scholarship to study at Skidmore College. I attempted to keep their hopes down because of my fear that

I might be denied a U.S. visa again, but they were more optimistic than I was. Mama Yawa was already dancing, and Amie was jumping up and down. Watta, Mama Yawa's youngest daughter, gave me a high five. I tried again to curb their excitement, but it was too late: the celebrations grew.

"Don't worry, my child," Mama Yawa said. "Tomorrow I will call on our ancestors. Your father knows the condition in which he left your moms, so he cannot sleep on us now. *Inshallah*, you will get that visa." She said "moms" because in Kissi tradition one's aunt is also regarded as one's mother.

Juxtaposing phrases like "God bless you" and "Inshallah" is normal in my Christian–Muslim family. Mama Yawa is a Catholic, but her husband is an Alhaji, and her children have a choice of both religions.

"Tout est dans la main de Dieu"—everything is in God's hand—my uncle, Docteur Saa Dimio, Mama Yawa's husband, uttered as his first contribution to the discussion. Docteur Saa Dimio always waits to have a separate conversation with me when everyone else is away. He doesn't like it when children interrupt him.

"Je vais te parler quand tous ces moustiques sont partis," he said. I will speak with you when these mosquitoes are gone.

Docteur Saa Dimio loves to refer to us as pests, especially when we are talkative. Sometimes his choice of animal metaphors upsets Mama Yawa. "Don't call my children piglets," she says.

Mama Yawa returned to the room, where I was still talking about Norway. She was smiling. "Mama Jeneba better wake up; her husband is about to go to the white man's land." She was talking about the spirit of my grandmother. Everyone in my family knew how much Mama Jeneba adored me as a child. If there is ever an ancestor to call upon to help me, she is number one on the list. Mama Yawa believes in the power of ancestors to intercede in earthly matters. I reckon there is no difference between the worship of Christ, who died and was resurrected, and the African belief in ancestors. Both beliefs center on the idea that death is not the end. One who believes that Christ died and rose in three days has no logical reason to condemn those who adhere to the belief that their dead relatives are roaming around them, receiving libations and offering blessings.

I went to bed that night thinking of the next day. I had no idea how the visa interview would turn out, but my major concern was how my mother and her sister would handle the news. I had borne setbacks before, and I was strong enough to handle another. My news of going to the U.S. made my family happy, but I was afraid that it might produce a terrible disappointment if this interview failed. My family would not understand how anyone could deny a visa to a student with a merit scholarship, but my experiences with visa applications had taught me that when it comes to the relationship between the West and the Rest, nothing can be taken for granted. Visas are sometimes denied to African dignitaries with no explanations, but Westerners often enter African countries with no visas.

The following morning, I woke up early and went outside. Mama Yawa was standing by the door. At first I wondered what she was doing, but I quickly realized that she was pouring libations for my ancestors and conjuring their spirits. I could not speak to her, because she could not respond to a mortal until the ceremony was completed. The ancestors would listen to her and respond to her intercession. She is an in-law to my ancestors, and they would listen to her on behalf of my mother, her younger sister. My ancestors are expected to remain faithful to their in-laws even in death. Both Mende and Kissi customs command that one does not deny the request of his in-law.

Traditional libations to the dead start with supplications to God Almighty, the most merciful and benevolent, overseer of the universe. A plea of forgiveness is offered to the dead, especially to those who died without offering their blessings for the family. The plea for forgiveness is followed by an explanation of the problem at hand. Sometimes people simply want to inform their deceased relative about special events in the family. After the information is given, a cup of water purified by *suras*, or Koranic verses, is poured into the earth to quench the thirst of the deceased as a request to transmit the supplications to God. When the libation is meant to invoke the ancestors for a special ceremony, alcoholic beverages are poured into the earth. Mama Yawa was rendering her prayers to God through my late father and grandmother.

I was one of the first people in line at the U.S. embassy. Mama Yawa, who would not let me go alone, stood by me. In my eagerness, I had forgotten to bring a passport photo. Mama Yawa and I had had to rush to Madina market so I could obtain one. Seeing the embassy police brought back memories of those in Oslo. The officer moved the X-ray baton up and down my body and admitted me to the waiting hall. The hall was less comfortable than the one in Oslo, and the number of people applying for visas was larger. Applicants were congested in a small waiting room, where we sat with our faces of despair, bargaining for an opportunity to go to the United States. There were mothers wishing to visit children they hadn't seen for years, businesspeople attempting to meet their partners, children whose parents had filed the application for them, tourists, and students like me. Even if we held valid papers, our eligibility was at the discretion of consular agents who were unconcerned with our individual needs.

"Joseph Kaifala, come in, please!" I heard my name on a megaphone. I walked through a metal detector, leaving my aunt in the waiting area. I went through a tiny hall leading to another waiting area for those selected for an interview.

"Are you Mr. Kaifala?" the lady behind the counter inquired with a smile.

"Yes," I replied with familiarity.

"We offer interviews in English, French, Soso, Fula, and Krio. Which language do you choose to be interviewed in?"

I was impressed by the choice of languages. A majority of Guineans only speak their native languages. "English," I said. It is what I had spoken for the last two years in Norway.

"I see you went to the UWC in Norway and want to go to the U.S.?" She got right down to business.

"Yes."

"Any relatives in the U.S.?"

"No."

"How do you intend to finance your education?" She looked at me.

"I have a full scholarship," I replied.

"Good for you." She smiled.

"Thanks." I smiled a little.

"How long are you going to be in the U.S.?"

"Four years," I replied.

"What is your intended major, Joseph?"

"International relations," I said.

"Wow. Planning on joining the UN?" she suggested.

I had always dreamed of working for UNHCR. "Yeah, I hope so," I replied with a wide smile.

"All right, Joseph. You qualify for a student visa to the United States. Your passport will be available at four p.m. today. It's been great meeting you. I wish you all the best in the States."

"Thank you so much," I said.

I walked back to the waiting room the same way I'd come in, smiling at a group of people waiting to be interviewed. Mama Yawa stood up as soon as I entered the room.

"A sorlaa?"—did you get it?—she asked in Kissi.

"Ae," I responded with a grin.

"Allah Nuwali," she repeated. Thanks be to God.

We spent the intervening hours waiting, and a little after four o'clock the consul walked into the waiting area with my passport.

"Congratulations, Joseph, and good luck."

I realized Mama Yawa wanted us to leave immediately, for fear of witchcraft and thieves. We used to hear rumors of people who were bewitched for a U.S. visa, or those who were attacked by bandits for their visa. I didn't think the people at the embassy presented any danger.

When we got home, I emailed the good news to Erik, Desiree, and Andreas. We were all happy that the visa obstacle was over. My main concern now was to get to the United States. Meanwhile, my passport made its way through the hands of relatives in the compound, albeit under Mama Yawa's ever-vigilant watch. My mother and Mama Yawa cracked jokes about how nervous they had been the night before. They lay in bed laughing at each other. My mother is not as overt in her expressions of faith as Mama Yawa, but I know she would have spent the night awake, reciting prayers.

We stayed up late, dancing, chatting, laughing, eating, and crying. A few days later, I said good-bye to everyone and left for Freetown by road. My mother prayed for me and wished me luck. The Conakry–Freetown highway was now safe to travel, but the trip required money, energy, and strength. The road was absolutely deplorable, full of vehicles overloaded with humans and goods and struggling under engines that barely functioned. Security forces on both sides of the border extracted as much money as possible from travelers. The illegal tariffs were worse than they had been when we passed though in 1998. The rainy season made the road dangerous; vehicles fell and rose into and out of potholes. But as dangerous as the road was, it was our best choice in a country that was recovering from a decade of war. We learn to endure the raucous and rickety conditions of our lives.

CHAPTER 20

With time, even a tortoise
makes it across the road.

I arrived safely in Freetown after a long and bumpy ride. I usually fall asleep during long trips, but I never sleep on the Guinea–Sierra Leone highway. This is not only because the roughness of the ride makes siestas impossible; it is also because I would rather be awake in the event of an emergency. The number of accident scenes we passed along the way was a reminder of the fragility of life on the Conakry–Freetown road during the rainy season. The roads were devastated, and drivers drove like they had spare lives when many did not even own spare tires.

"Driver take time o!" a frightened passenger screamed as we were jolted like spiritual dancers. Drivers were not always successful at dodging potholes. Sometimes passengers disembarked from the vehicle to venture on foot across large puddles and fragile bridges. On segments of the road where the tarmac had endured beyond expectation, my fellow passengers and I returned to discussing whatever topic was exciting at the moment.

I always take a Peugeot 504 when traveling between Conakry and Freetown. It is less durable and spacious than a minivan and so cannot be desperately overloaded with heavy cargo. Still, drivers of Peugeots fill every crevice capable of holding anything. We sometimes drove past other Peugeots that were loaded to the brim and leaned to one side like a dilapidated wall. These mobile caskets often bore inscriptions: "God's Time Is the Best," "Mother's Blessings," "Long Life," "Fear Judgment Day," and so on. In countries where there are no laws, poor people die as they live—poorly. Those who fear the looming possibility of unwarranted death cannot survive in many African countries. Our clash with mortality begins the very day we are born. Calamities like armed conflicts and natural disasters only exacerbate the misery of our existence, leaving us in an even greater dystopia. But somehow we survive.

My brother and uncle were eager to know the outcome of my interview.

"Fellow, do you have the visa?" Francis asked, hesitantly.

He gave me a satisfactory smile as if he had held no doubt that I would get the visa. My brother understood both my disappointment over my failure to obtain a visa in Oslo and the anxiety I'd felt about my next attempt. A few years prior, he had been granted a UWC scholarship to both Lester Pearson UWC in Canada and UWC Adriatic in Italy but had gone to neither because unlike me, when he was denied a Canadian visa after so much effort, he had had enough. He refused to pursue an Italian visa and enrolled instead at home, at Fourah Bay College in Freetown.

Barbara Opitz, international student adviser at Skidmore College, booked my flight on SN Brussels. I told her my intended major, and she registered me for classes. I was enrolled in a writing seminar, Critical Issues in World Politics, African Religions, and a first-year seminar called Human Dilemmas, which would become one of my favorite classes at Skidmore.

I went to the SN Brussels office in Freetown so the airline could verify that my travel documents were in order. I had previously met Sally, the agent at the airline's Wilberforce Street office, while planning my trip to Norway. She remembered me and was happy to see me. However, she gave me the bad news that the visa in my possession was not an F-1, a student visa; rather, it was a B-2, a visitor's visa. Somehow the embassy in Conakry had issued me the wrong visa. The B-2 would permit me to travel to the U.S. but would have left me ineligible for school. It was a rainy day in Freetown. Francis and I ran to the U.S. embassy, which was located near the Freetown Cotton Tree. The embassy staff offered two options: "You can either go back to Conakry or we can mail your passport to you."

I selected the latter. I did not have the strength or money to return to Conakry. And the mistake was their fault, not mine. If they had insisted that I return to Conakry, which they could have, I would have found a way. But they didn't insist. I waited in Freetown for another week.

During that time, we were evicted from the house on Andrew Street. Americans like to say, "When it rains, it pours." I felt like I was caught in a monsoon. The eviction arose from various disagreements between my aunt and the landlords. The rent was low, but my aunt had deliberately allowed the house to fall into disrepair. One of the most significant problems was Auntie Ade's refusal to repair the roof. The corroded zinc had disintegrated into tatters, and Auntie Ade expected the landlords to repair it, which they declined to do. I understood the landlords' position: the rent was too low for them to also undertake repairs. My uncle was spending more time in Lungi, and my aunt wanted to move close to her mother on Congo Cross. This was the real reason she failed to perform maintenance on the building.

Auntie Ade invited my brother and me to move to Congo Cross with her (our uncle had left on a trip to Guinea shortly after my return), but we knew that was not a workable invitation. She had always wanted to get rid of us, but our uncle was adamant that we stay with him. My uncle considered my brother and me his children, and he was unwilling to relinquish what he saw as his responsibility to take care of us. I persuaded the landlords, who were our neighbors and friends, to allow me to remain in the empty house until I received my passport. I slept on an old mattress on the floor of what used to be my room.

My passport was returned on time, but unfortunately I missed my flight to Brussels. Lungi International Airport is separated from mainland Freetown by the sea, requiring transport by either a helicopter or a government-run ferry. An expensive helicopter flight was not an option for me. The government ferries are cheaper but unreliable. On any given day, they might be broken or simply not running because they failed to book a full load (an excessive load, really) of passengers and vehicles. One of the ferries was out of service on the day of my flight, and another was docked at the terminal, empty. In corrupt and mismanaged countries, citizens don't deserve an explanation for services withheld.

I decided to travel by a third method—the people's method: a rickety fishing canoe or a crude speedboat with an unreliable engine. These two transportation options are made available by enterprising operators whenever the ferries are out of service. Everything is possible in Sierra Leone, but nothing is certain, and that is the extent of our development. There is always an alternative. The only question is, what sacrifices are we willing to make?

I settled for an overloaded canoe, but I got to the airport too late to board my flight, even though it had not yet taken off. Lungi Airport had no automated X-ray machines at the time. I arrived a few minutes after the manual check-in had closed, and although my suitcase was only a little larger than a carry-on, I was deemed unsafe to board. I had to wait in Lungi until SN Brussels' next flight from the airport: four days later.

I went to the nearby town of Tintafor, where my uncle was temporarily based as a high school teacher. He was in Guinea, and I didn't know his address, but I found it with the help of an *okada* (motorbike taxi) operator who knew him.

I had not anticipated another last-minute problem, but in every situation, *l'homme propose, Dieu dispose*. Mishaps like the ones that were happening to me are the sorts of things that make people believe in witchcraft. I could have easily settled on the idea that my enemies had bewitched me and offered whatever animal sacrifice was suggested by a marabout, but I believe that sometimes things go wrong and human beings don't understand each other's woes. I could not know why the U.S. embassy in Conakry had issued me the wrong visa, why the ferries were not working, why the canoe was so slow to get across, why I was prevented from boarding my flight even though the plane stood on the runway for another hour. Maybe I was unlucky—unless, of course, God was with me in my anguish and was protecting me in ways I could not understand. My only certainty was that I had a visa and a ticket to Amaika.

I spent my four days in Tintafor sleeping, taking walks, and sleeping some more. On the day of my next scheduled departure, I was, for obvious reasons, the first passenger at the airport. I ordered a meal and a large Carlsberg at the airport restaurant. On September 16, 2004, I boarded SN Brussels to Belgium en route to the United States. I was a couple of weeks late for the semester, but I was happy to finally be on my way to Amaika, my home for the next four years.

I thought of my mother, who always prays for her children in the silence of her night. I reflected on the love of Mama Jeneba and her faith in the power of education. I thought of Ben M. Kaifala, my beloved father.

> To be a man is not easy.
> So hold your tears!
> Hold your tears!

ACKNOWLEDGMENTS

A memoir is necessarily the life of others. Many of you have traveled this road with me. Thank you for the contributions you made to my life. Without you, I may not have survived to write this book. Since we all manage traumatic moments differently, I have left out stories involving others I believe should not be told without explicit permission from them. I have also omitted details I believe could be emotionally damaging to others.

I am grateful for the contributions of my beloved brother, Francis Kaifala, Esq. I am proud of what we have achieved together. A special love for my sisters, Amie Kaifala and Hawa Kaifala-Samba. To my brother Sahr Kendema, for your ability to recall only the embarrassing stories of our childhood—bringing a pinch of humility to stories that may sometimes appear heroic. Francis got married and brought me a sister I love dearly. This writer appreciates a new girl who is too polite to ignore him. In gratitude, Dunia Kaifala, I will always be the celebrity who sits on your floor.

I am particularly indebted to Musa Adams Tongi, Augustine Samba, Christopher A. Jamiru, Doris Jamiru, Mathew Kaifala, Jeneba Lamin, Sisi Jeneba, Sisters Joan and Marceline, Fr. Emmanuel Etienne, Keifa Tongi, Adama Kounateh, Abraham Kounateh, Mohamed Kounateh, Brima Kounateh, Christiana Tongi, Brima Foday, Alex Bindi, June Taylor, and sister Tuku. To my grandmothers, Kona Sandouno, Lobou Sandouno, Mama Jeneba, and late Grandpa Vandy Tongi. In memory of my beloved uncle Mohamed Lord Vandy Tongi and my aunts Rosaline Sandouno and Finda Marie Tolno. Thank you to Vieux Sandouno of Gueckedou. To my lovely aunt Fatu Tolno and her children.

A special love for my Aberdeen family: Dr. Jowo Aberdeen, Miniratu Aberdeen, Kadie Aberdeen, Alhaji Oshoba Aberdeen, Saudatu, Salma, Fatima, Ibu, Mommy, Ibrahim Sesay, Mahawa, Memuna, and my late brother, Olu. I know Olu would have carried this book around telling everyone how proud he is. To my cousins, Ben Kaifala, Fatmata Mansaray, and John and Edmond Kettor.

I maintain a special place in my heart for my uncle Sahr J. Tolno. You are, as my mother said, a father to me. My academic achievements are in your honor. Much love for Aunty Ade Tolno, Aunty Elizabeth, Joseph, Valery, Pascal, Rose, and Sia Tolno. To Hawa and Emilia Tongi, Adam, Patrick, and Isaac Tongi. In gratitude to George Sandouno, my coolest uncle, and the Bainda, Lewis, Cole, Manley, Macaulay, Williams, Pratt, and Taylor families of Murray Town.

The finest place in my heart is reserved for my mother, Tewa Kaifala, the woman who loved my eccentric father. Your love and strength have made this book possible. This is also for the love and support of Finda Angeline Tolno and her husband, Saa Dimio Sandouno. Much love to my cousins Tibab, Mariata, Borbor, and Watta. For Isatu and lovely Yeabeh Jalloh, Musa Bainda, Miltina Ndaloma, Brima, Haja, Sally, Hawa, Daddy, Mohamed, Alhaji, and Hawa Bainda.

Some friends are brothers, and that is what I have found in Abdo Assad. I am proud of your work and the young family you are growing. Thank you, Josephine Assad, for your love. Thank you to Musu Mary Sankoh, Karimata Bah, Alicia Wells Day, Jeremy Day, Luis and Rebecca Salmaso, Rick and Tamar Wells, Martha Blackall Bunker, Ida Rose Nininger, Chernor and Aissatou Bah, Alyssa May LaPane, Danielle McCourt, James Omo Oloye, Charlee Bianchini, Catherine Cantwell, Katie R. Thomas, Shannon Clarke, Jonathan John, Ibrahim Jalloh, Sweta Parbhakah, Jess Wilkerson, Billy Peard, Kristian Ngombu, Federica D'alessandra, Peter S. Brock, Richard Lee, Prof. Stephanie Farrior, Miriam Lieberman, and my entire SkidFam. I remain grateful to David and Rebecca Walker, A. J. Lasite, Aseem Shrivastava, Maria Teresa Julianello, Fatmata

Jalloh-Chamberlain, Abdinnah Jalloh, Imani and Elijah Koroma, Mohamed, Abdulrahman, Alhassan and Memuna Jalloh, Daniel and Barbara Toa-kwapong, Alistair and Lesley Robertson, Peter and Lesley Wilson, Mariano Giampietri, Isabell Bolander, Talha Khan, Horacio Diaz, Tormod Carlsen, Kipsy Ndwandwe, Niko Brauer, Siim Soplepmann, Bastian Aue, Bo Rong, Gifty Amiah, Matilda Walker, Deborah Bombo, Victor Moiwo, Thomas George, Chernor Barry, Leonard Gordon, Andreas Kokkvoll Tveit, Elizabeth and Esther Bundor, Yaya Sidi Sackor, Fayia Porter, Carol Springs, Mary-Beth O'Brien, Roy Ginsberg, and Ms. Edna Jones.

All this I owe to Professor Michael Marx. You were the first to make me realize that these stories could contribute to my desire to make the world better every day, and you taught me the patience to write. I am equally grateful to your family, my family, Prof. Catherine Golden-Marx, and Jesse and Emmet Golden-Marx. I extend a great deal of love and appreciation to Prof. Kate Graney, Sean, Ronan, and Mimi; Barbara Opitz, Darren Drabek, Sadiatu Marrah, Robert Coleman, and the entire Skidmore Dining Hall staff. In gratitude to Dandora Tongi for the love you have for my brother and me. I could not have achieved many things in the U.S. without the love of Martin and Jean Shafiroff; Elizabeth and Jackie Shafiroff; Catherine Bertini; Judith Goldstein; Erik, Martin, Nils, Björn, Elin, and Frida Bolmstrand; Ulla and Magnus Bolmstrand; Nikolai Barnwell; Vijay Ramesh; Henrienke Prins; Leonor and Hugo Krawczyk; Adi Cohen; Nir, Noa, and Liat Krawczyk—mother of the Jeneba Project mascot, Milai. With special love for my Norwegian family: Desiree Ovretveit, Inge Larsen, Anna Kamilla, Elias, Jakob, Johannes, Ole Johannes Ovretveit, and all the good folks of Sande. Many thanks for the folks at Turner Publishing, especially my good friend Stephanie Bowman and Jon O'Neal.

In special honor of those who were imprisoned with me. The strength you demonstrated in those horrific days gives me zeal to carry on. To those who never made it or have now died, this is a memorial to you.